STRATEGIC PRAYER MANUAL

The Weapon for Effective Leadership

ALFRETA ELMORE WOODS

ISBN 9781562295110

Christian Living Books, Inc.
P.O. Box 7584
Largo, MD 20792
christianlivingbooks.com
We bring your dreams to fruition.

First Edition

Library of Congress Cataloging-in-Publication Data

Identifiers: LCCN 2021026856 (print) | LCCN 2021026857 (ebook)
Classification: LCC BV210.3 .W665 2021 (print) | LCC BV210.3 (ebook) | DDC 248.3/2--dc23
LC record available at https://lccn.loc.gov/2021026856
LC ebook record available at https://lccn.loc.gov/2021026857

CONTENTS

FOREWORD

As a servant of Christ and His church, I have grown to understand how vital prayer is in every aspect of the church—from the pulpit to the pew. *The Strategic Prayer Manual* is a practical guide that will equip you to engage in effective, fervent prayer for your church, leaders, and ministry. This manual will help align your heart with God as you pray His Word and will over your church.

—Dr. Adron Robinson
Senior Pastor
Hillcrest Baptist Church

THE LORD'S PRAYER

Our Father, which art in heaven,
Hallowed be thy name. Thy
kingdom come, Thy will be
done in earth, as it is in heaven.
Give us this day our daily bread.
And forgive us our debts, as
we forgive our debtors. And
lead us not into temptation, but
deliver us from evil: For thine
is the kingdom, and the power,
and the glory, for ever. Amen.

Matthew 6:9-13, KJV

INTRODUCTION

THIS MANUAL IS DEDICATED to the leadership of Broadview Missionary Baptist Church. I wrote it in appreciation to my BMBC family who played such an integral part in my Christian education and development. This is my way of saying, "Thank you, BMBC family, for all that you have done and continue to do in my life." I will always keep you in my thoughts and prayers.

The primary purpose of this prayer manual is to guide church leaders as they pray for others, specifically their respective ministries. Praise God for inspiring and guiding me into the ministry of intercession. This journey has taken me to Television 38 where I received two years of formal training as a prayer counselor, to Living Word Christian Center (LWCC) where I learned prayer strategies and how to travail in prayer, and to Moody Bible Institute where I was taught the theology of prayer. That theology starts with the model Jesus gave us known as The Lord's Prayer:

The Lord's Prayer Concepts

- I cannot pray "Our Father, which art in heaven" if all of my interests and pursuits only concern earthly things

- I cannot pray "Hallowed be Thy name, Thy kingdom come, Thy will be done" if I am only seeking to please myself and do my own thing

- I cannot pray "In earth as it is in heaven, give us this day our daily bread, and forgive us our debts as we forgive our debtors" if I continue to hold a grudge against anyone.

- I cannot pray "And lead us not into temptation, but deliver us from evil" if I am not willing to fight evil with my life and prayers.

- I cannot pray "For Thine is the kingdom, and the power, and the glory, forever. Amen" unless I can put my prayers into the hands of Jesus and trust Him with everything.

During my tenure at Moody, I was taught prayer discipline. I learned how to pray conversational prayers. I also learned that prayer must be a *lifestyle.* That discipline has certainly developed my prayer life and has taken my prayers to another level. I pray that you will glean from my experience and instruction.

Chapter 1

WHAT IS PRAYER?

> *If my people, which are called by my name, shall humble themselves, and pray, and seek my face, and turn from their wicked ways; then will I hear from heaven, and will forgive their sin, and will heal their land. (2 Chronicles 7:14, KJV)*

G OD HAS ONE VEHICLE and two methods to advance the kingdom of God on the earth. The one vehicle is the church of Jesus Christ. The two methods are prayer and the proclamation of the gospel. Christians are to pray for the church, families, and communities. We must pray for our governments, kings, all those in authority and proclaim the gospel of Jesus Christ to everyone.

Prayer is the attitude of our hearts toward God. The children of God have a natural desire to pour out their souls to the Lord, cry out to heaven, draw near to God, kneel in humble submission before the Father, and seek His face. *Fellowship with God is the heart of prayer.* Too often we lose sight of the simplicity of prayer.

- Prayer is a vital key that connects us with our heavenly Father
- Prayer is both an incredible privilege and an awesome responsibility
- Prayer can move the hand of God in situations where there is no hope
- Prayer is crying out to God from the depths of our hearts
- Prayer is the pouring out of our souls to God

The key to answered prayer is praying in accordance with *God's will* and *His Word.* Prayer is not seeking our own will but aligning ourselves with the will of God. The Bible contains many examples of prayer and exhortations to pray.

My house shall be called the house of prayer. (Matthew 21:13a)

God's people must be people of prayer. Prayer can be audible or silent, private or public, formal or informal. All prayer(s) must be offered in faith, in the name of the Lord Jesus Christ, and by the power of the Holy Spirit.

Prayer Is the Way Christians Communicate with God

Prayer is the primary way for believers in Jesus Christ to express their emotions and desires to God and fellowship with Him. We pray to praise and thank God, as well as tell Him how much we love Him. We pray to God to enjoy His presence, tell Him what is going on in our lives, and make our requests known unto Him.

We pray to seek God's guidance, wisdom, and forgiveness. God loves these exchanges with His children just as we love the exchanges we have with our children.

Prayer is not our passport to heaven—Jesus is. Prayer is a conversation between you and God. He gives you His phone number:

> *Call unto me, and I will answer thee, and shew thee great and mighty things, which thou knowest not.* (Jeremiah 33:3, KJV)

Emergency numbers may be dialed directly. No operator assistance is necessary. All lines are open to heaven 24 hours a day! Just fifteen minutes spent in the presence of God can change your life forever!

Prayer Is a Dialogue between the Believer and God

Prayer is a two-way communication that requires both talking and listening. It is not complete if we do all the talking and expect God to do all the listening. We should pray and listen to God's voice, which means being ready to hear and obey Him. As said earlier, our heavenly Father does not speak just to give people a chance to decide if they want to obey Him. He also speaks to those who take Him seriously and stand ready to respond to whatever He says. Let us learn to talk to God and listen to His voice.

Prayer Is for Our Benefit

We need a relationship with God, which is available to us through Jesus Christ. This is obtained primarily through our engagement in prayer. We function best when we are in a proper relationship with God. The most basic definition of prayer is *talking to God*. Prayer gives you direct access to God; it is the human soul communicating with God (the Creator of our souls).

Prayer Is Directed to God the Father

In the New Testament, Christian prayer is addressed to God the Father and in the name of Jesus Christ, our Mediator. It is only through Christ and the enabling grace of the indwelling Holy Spirit that we can approach the Father. Jesus did not say to pray to Him. We must pray to God the Father and close in Jesus' name. God the Father is the Head of the Godhead and Jesus Christ, the Son of God, is the Second Person of the Godhead. Therefore, we pray in respect to God, address our prayers to the Father, and close them in Jesus' name.

Prayer Should Be Like Breathing

Breathing is natural. When we are born into the family of God, we enter His presence and commune with Him. As believers, we have the privilege of going to Him in prayer. Unfortunately, many believers hold their *spiritual breath* for long periods thinking brief moments with God are sufficient for them to survive. Such restrictions of their spiritual intake are usually caused by sinful desires. The fact is that to be fully functional, every believer must continually be in the presence of God, constantly breathing in His truths.

Prayer to the Father

Heavenly Father, in the name of Jesus, we thank You that through the indwelling of Your Holy Spirit, we can come boldly to Your throne of grace. We thank You that as we allow Your Holy Spirit to pray through and for us (according to Your will and Your Word) we are building up ourselves by our most holy faith. Help us to learn to pray sincerely with the expectation that our prayers will be answered.

Thank You, Lord Jesus, for Your love for us. Help us to forever draw nearer to You. Let the words of our mouths and the meditation of our hearts be acceptable in Your sight forever. You are our Lord, our strength, and our Redeemer. In Jesus' name, we pray. Amen!

What Should We Pray For?

God commands us to pray with confidence and in accordance with His will. God's Word is His will. Therefore, we should pray for the things for which the Bible commands us to pray. We are told to pray for our enemies, for God to send missionaries, and that we do not enter into temptation. We are to pray for ministers of the gospel, government officials, relief from affliction, and healing of the land.

We should pray God's Holy Word with faith because His Word will not return unto Him void. It will accomplish what He pleases and will achieve the purpose for which it was sent (Isaiah 55:11). When we meditate on God's Word and hide it in our hearts, we will not sin against God (Psalm 119:11). When we pray in faith proclaiming His Holy Word, we are assured that we please Him, and He will reward us.

We should pray for the salvation of lost souls and all leaders in every capacity—everyone. We should pray for God's kingdom to come and His will be done on the earth as it is in heaven (Matthew 6:11).

Why Should We Pray?

We should pray because we are believers in Christ. He is our role model; therefore, we should follow His example. Jesus communed daily with His Father through prayer. If He, being the Second Person of the Godhead, needed to commune with His Father, surely, all of us do.

We should also pray to:

- Convey our reverence unto the Lord
- Receive wisdom and guidance
- Stay connected to the Spirit of the living God
- Maintain a fresh anointing in our lives

- Intercede for others
- Remain in fellowship with God
- Overcome when things look helpless and hopeless
- Maintain spiritual discipline and reverence to God
- Have perfect and complete oneness with God
- Express the ultimate aspect of thankfulness God requires of us
- Avoid falling into temptation
- Ask for direction and wisdom

Prayer Is an Effective Weapon for Spiritual Warfare

The Christian walks by faith, not by sight. Therefore, the weapons of spiritual warfare must be known, recognized, understood, and appropriated (taken possession of). The Holy Spirit places great emphasis on them. The weapons of warfare are listed below.

- The gospel – this is the greatest weapon of spiritual warfare because when accepted by the unbeliever, it transfers that person from the kingdom of darkness into the kingdom of light
- The blood of Jesus
- Faith – empowers prayer
- Your faith confessions (the shield of faith) – these are your faith-filled words, spoken aloud from the applied Word of God over another person, self, or circumstances
- Prayer
- The Word of God
- Agreeing in prayer

Prayer Thought – *Fellowship with God is the heart of prayer.*

Scripture: 1 John 5:14-15; 2 Chronicles 32:20; Ephesians 3:14, 6:18; James 1:6, 4:3; John 16:23; Jude 1:20-21; Luke 11:1, 18:1; Mark 11:17; Psalm 10:4, 73:28; Romans 8:26, 12:12

Binding and Loosing

The word "bind" means to tie up. The word "loose" means to untie. Therefore, you do not bind and loose the spirit that is afflicting the person. Rather, you bind the spirit and loose the person from the spirit that is afflicting him.

> *Verily I say unto you, Whatsoever ye shall bind on earth shall be bound in heaven: and whatsoever ye shall loose on earth shall be loosed in heaven.* (Matthew 18:18)

It is exactly the same as saying, "Lord, I humbly recognize Your sovereignty and petition You to give me this job in accordance with Your will." You decree something to be simply by saying it. Declaring it causes it to happen because your words are seeds. Understand that it is not happening by your power but by the power and authority of God (who resides in you). You can simply say, "Lord, I petition You to give me favor in the job interview and that I will be hired for that job if it is Your will."

Scripture: *1 John 1:6-7, 3:22, 5:14; 1 Peter 2:9; 1 Thessalonians 5:5; Ephesians 5:8, 6:11-17; Hebrews 11:1; James 1:6-7, 4:7; John 12:46; Job 22:28; Luke 10:17; Matthew 4:1-11, 7:7, 16:17-18; Mark 11:23-24; Proverbs 18:21, 23:7; Psalm 2:7; Revelation 12:11; Romans 4:17*

Where Should We Pray?

Do you have a place where you can pray alone? Do you have that secret place where you can rest in the shadow of the Almighty? Do you have a place where you meet with the Lord alone? I pray you do, but if you do not, I encourage you to find it. God wants you to come to Him in secret and share your heart with Him. You can tell Him any and everything. He is your best friend!

The greatest part is He can make wrong things right in every way.

> And we know that all things work together for good to them that love God, to them who are the called according to His purpose.
>
> (Romans 8:28, KJV)

No matter what you are going through in your relationship, whether you have problems with the kids, work, money, health, whatever. Jesus is there for you. He loves you and is available to you 24/7.

Is There A Best Place to Pray?

Have a quiet prayer place where you can communicate with heaven without earthly disturbances. It does not matter where you pray, God will listen. However, a place of serenity reduces distractions and helps you to focus on your communion with Him. God understands us more than we can ever know.

> Now Peter and John went up together into the temple at the hour of prayer, being the ninth hour. (Acts 3:1, KJV)

Notice three significant things about the preceding Scripture verse:

- There is a prayer partner
- There is a prayer place
- There is a prayer time

You can pray anywhere. For some, it might be in a favorite room or a certain chair. Others may have a special table or prefer to pray in their vehicles. Some may like praying while sitting on a bench in the park. Wherever you choose to talk with God, He will hear you. The location is insignificant. Most important is that you take the time to pray. It does not matter where you pray, God will listen. He understands us more than we can ever know.

> For we do not have a high priest who cannot sympathize with our weaknesses, but One who has been tempted in all things as we are, yet without sin. Therefore, let us draw near with confidence to the

Prayer Thought – *Labor with God in prayer until you get a breakthrough!*

Scripture: *2 Thessalonians 3:1; Colossians 4:2-3; Isaiah 55:11; James 5:13; Luke 10:2, 4:3; Matthew 5:44, 6:10, 26:41; Psalm 119:11; Romans 8:26-27*

throne of grace, so that we may receive mercy and find grace to help in time of need. (Hebrews 4:15-16, KJV)

I pray that you will find your quiet place!

Where Did People of the Bible Pray?

Throughout the Bible, we see that the saints were not limited to praying in any specific location. They prayed in various places as seen below:

In Private and Alone

But when you pray, go into your room, close the door and pray to the Father who is unseen. Then Your Father, who sees what is done in secret, will reward you. (Matthew 6:6, GNT)

Very early in the morning, while it was still dark, Jesus got up, left the house and went off to a solitary place, where he prayed. (Mark 1:35, CSB)

But Jesus often withdrew to lonely places and prayed. (Luke 5:16, NIV)

One of those days Jesus went out to a mountainside to pray and spent the night praying to God. (Luke 6:12, NIV)

About noon the following day as they were on their journey and approaching the city, Peter went up on the roof to pray. (Acts 10:9, NIV)

In Bed

On my bed I remember you; I think of you through the watches of the night. (Psalm 63:6, NIV)

At the River

On the Sabbath we went outside the city gate to the river, where we expected to find a place of prayer. We sat down and began to speak to the women who had gathered there. (Acts 16:13, NIV)

On the Sea Shore

When it was time to leave, we left and continued on our way. All of them, including wives and children, accompanied us out of the city, and there on the beach we knelt to pray. (Acts 21:5, NIV)

At the Well

Then he prayed, LORD, God of my master Abraham, make me successful today, and show kindness to my master Abraham. 13 See, I am standing beside this spring, and the daughters of the townspeople are coming out to draw water. (Genesis 24:12-13, NIV)

In God's House

There was also a prophetess, Anna, the daughter of Phanuel, of the tribe of Asher. She was very old she had lived with her husband seven years after her marriage, and then was a widow until she was eighty-four. She never left the temple but worshiped night and day, fasting and praying. (Luke 2:36-37, NIV)

On the Battlefield

Praying always with all prayer and supplication in the Spirit, being watchful to this end with all perseverance and supplication for all the saints and for me. (Ephesians 6:10-20, NKJV)

They cried out to God in the battle. He heeded their prayer because they put their trust in Him. (1 Chronicles 5:20, NKJV)

Prayer Thought – *When in doubt, pray; let prayer be your spiritual guide.*

Scripture: *1 Timothy 4:4–5; Colossians 4:2; Deuteronomy 4:7; Ephesians 5:19-20; Hebrews 4:16; James 4:8; Jeremiah 42:1; Luke 11:9-10; Matthew 18:19-20; Philippians 4:6; Psalm 116:12, 17, 145:18.*

When Should We Pray?

We should pray at all times because it is a means of communicating with God, which is vital. We pray expecting to receive what we desire! It does not mean we have to stay on our knees 24 hours a day. It simply means in all of our ways, we should acknowledge (consult with) God.

The apostle Paul commands us to "Pray without ceasing!" Paul is not referring to non-stop talking but an attitude of God-consciousness and God-surrender that we carry with us all the time. Every moment is to be lived in the awareness that God is with us. He is actively involved and engaged in our thoughts and actions. When our thoughts turn to worry, fear, discouragement, and anger, we are to consciously and quickly turn them into prayer and every prayer into thanksgiving.

> *But in everything, through prayer and petition with thanksgiving, present your requests to God.* (Philippians 4:6, CSB)

Paul taught the believers at Colossae to devote themselves to prayer being watchful and thankful. He exhorted the Ephesian believers to see prayer as a weapon for fighting spiritual battles.

> *As we go through the day, prayer should be our first response and our last response to every situation. Pray alone. Let prayer be the key of the morning and the bolt at night. The best way to fight against sin is to fight on our knees.* — Philip Henry

Will you commit today to pray harder, longer, and more frequently than ever?

> *The effectual fervent prayer of a righteous man availeth much.*
> (James 5:16, KJV)

What Prayer Is Not

Prayer Is Not Magic

We cannot summon God as though He is a genie waiting to grant all of our wishes without regard for our circumstances or the consequences.

Prayer Is Not a Demand

While we can make requests of God in prayer, we dare not make demands. God is the Creator of the universe and does not take orders from us.

Prayer Is Not a Guarantee Against Suffering

I have told you these things, so that in me you may have peace. In this world you will have trouble. But take heart! I have overcome the world.

(John 16:33, NIV)

Dear friends, do not be surprised at the fiery ordeal that has come on you to test you, as though something strange were happening to you. But rejoice inasmuch as you participate in the sufferings of Christ, so that you may be overjoyed when his glory is revealed. (1 Peter 4:12-13, NIV)

Prayer Is Not an Opportunity for Us to Show Off

And when thou prayest, thou shalt not be as the hypocrites, for they love to pray standing in the synagogues and in the corners of the streets, so they may be seen of men. Verily I say unto you, they have their reward. (Matthew 6:5, KJV)

How Should We Pray?

God hates pride. Therefore, we should pray in humility to our heavenly Father in Jesus' name. Praying in Jesus' name acknowledges that no one can come unto the Father except through His Son Jesus Christ. We should ask God for forgiveness of our sins committed by omission and commission. In doing so, we acknowledge our offenses against others whether known or unknown. We should pray in faith and never waiver because a doubleminded man is unstable in all his ways

> **Prayer Thought** – *Praying without ceasing unto God causes us to depend on God's grace rather than upon ourselves.*
>
> *Scripture: 1 Thessalonians 5:17; Colossians 4:2; Ephesians 6:18; Philippians 4:6*

(James 1:8). Our prayers should be unselfish. In other words, we must not only pray for our families and ourselves, but we should also pray for others sincerely.

The effectual, fervent prayers of the righteous man, availeth much.
(James 5:16, KJV)

Principles of Effective Prayer

All prayers must be directed to the Father – Our minds and hearts must be focused on God the Father. And as said earlier, we should ask in Jesus' name. Before you pray, yield to the Holy Spirit in the name of Jesus Christ and ask Him to lead you with faith-filled words. Back your prayers with faith (trust in Jesus Christ). Your faith moves God's heart and hand to act on your behalf.

Your faith must be unwavering – Reject doubt and unbelief. It takes the same effort to believe as it does not to. You choose. Faith is a decision; you decide if you will believe and stand on your faith or not.

Speak your prayers aloud – Your faith-filled words (faith confession spoken under the anointing) are spiritual power packets. When your prayers are in line with God's will and His Word, they move the Holy Spirit to come into agreement with them. He waters these seeds of faith (your words) and empowers you by bringing forth the evidence of things unseen (things from the Spirit-realm into the physical realm).

Now faith is the substance of things hoped for the evidence of things not seen. (Hebrews 11:1, KJV)

To have an effective prayer life, we must:
- Pray in the name of Jesus (through Him as the Mediator)
- Pray according to the will of God
- Pray in faith
- Pray with humility and respect for God
- Repent of sin and seek God's forgiveness

For prayer to be effectual, it must be made through intercession. It must be per-severing, genuine prayer; for example, Jacob wrestled all night in prayer with God. Effectual prayer is offered up with the agony of desire. If we are to pray effectively, consistently, and with dedication, we must offer up our prayers in Jesus' name. We cannot prevail in prayer without renouncing our sins. Pray in faith and expect God to do what He said He would do.

What to Do Before You Pray

- Confess and renounce your sins
- Purge yourself with the blood of Jesus
- Ask for the fire of the Holy Spirit to come upon you
- Forgive all those who have offended you
- Pray for at least half an hour per day
- Pray before doing anything
- Study the Bible daily
- Pray fervently without ceasing

Five Keys to Effective Prayers

Use the five keys outlined below and as depicted in the "prayer hand" illustration.

Praise – Start with praise to God and express your reverence for Him.

Thanksgiving – Thank God for sending His Son Jesus to die for your sins. Thank God for being with you and providing for your family. Thank God for His great, unconditional love (Ephesians 5:20).

Intercession – Pray for others (Ephesians 6:18-19).

Prayer Thought – *Put God first, and He will direct your path and steer you in the right direction.*

Scripture: 1 Corinthians 10:30-31; 1 Thessalonians 5:17; Daniel 6:10; Ephesians 6:18; Luke 18:1; Proverbs 3:5-9

Confession – Ask God to forgive your sins (1 John 1:9). James 5:16 says to confess your sins to each other and pray for one another that you may be healed. The earnest prayer of a righteous person has great power and produces wonderful results.

Petition – Present your needs and requests to God (1 Samuel 1:27). Close with thanking and praising God for specific provisions and blessings.

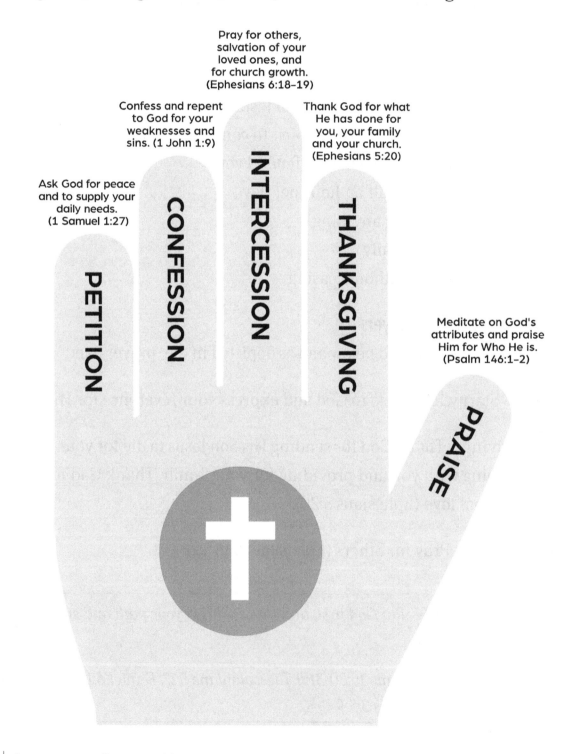

Pray for others, salvation of your loved ones, and for church growth. (Ephesians 6:18–19)

Confess and repent to God for your weaknesses and sins. (1 John 1:9)

Thank God for what He has done for you, your family and your church. (Ephesians 5:20)

Ask God for peace and to supply your daily needs. (1 Samuel 1:27)

Meditate on God's attributes and praise Him for Who He is. (Psalm 146:1–2)

PETITION

CONFESSION

INTERCESSION

THANKSGIVING

PRAISE

Hindrances to a Powerful Prayer Life

There are many hindrances that may prevent us from having powerful prayer lives. As a result, our prayers to God are not always heard. Let us turn our attention to a few of the most obvious hindrances and ways to deal with each of them.

Unconfessed Sin Hinders Prayer

The most obvious hindrance to a powerful prayer life is the presence of unconfessed sin in the hearts of the one who is praying. Such a restriction exists between God and us when we come to Him with unconfessed sins in our lives.

> *But your iniquities have separated you from your God; your sins have hidden his face from you, so that he will not hear.* (Isaiah 59:2, NIV)

David concurred, knowing from experience that God is far from those who try to hide their sins:

> *If I regard iniquity (sin) in my heart, the Lord will not hear me.*
> (Psalm 66:18, KJV)

Scripture: Isaiah 59:2; James 4:1-5; John 17

Selfishness Hinders Prayer

You ask and do not receive because you ask with the wrong motives, so you may spend it on your pleasures. Examine yourself. Make sure your prayers are not motivated by selfish desires. Living according to selfish, fleshly desires will hinder your prayers because it produces a hard heart toward others. If you find selfishness is a reason for unanswered prayers, confess your selfishness to God and repent.

Scripture: Isaiah 59:2; James 4:3, 5:8, 16; Psalm 66:18

Unforgiveness Toward Others Hinders Prayer

When we refuse to forgive others, the roots of bitterness grow up in our hearts and choke our prayers. How can we expect God to pour out His blessings upon us if we harbor hatred and bitterness toward others? This principle is illustrated in the parable of the unforgiving servant. The story teaches that God has forgiven us for debt beyond measure (our sin). He expects us to forgive others as we have been forgiven. To refuse to do so will hinder our prayers.

> *Scripture: Mark 11:25-26; Matthew 6:14-15*

Doubt Hinders Prayer

Another major hindrance to effective prayer is doubt (unbelief). Praying without doubt means praying in faith. When we come to God in prayer, doubting His character, purpose, and promises will hinder our prayers.

> *But without faith it is impossible to please him: for he that cometh to God must believe that he is, and that he is a rewarder of them that diligently seek him.* (Hebrews 11:6, KJV)

Our confidence must be in God's ability to grant any request in accordance with His will and purpose for our lives.

> *But let him ask in faith, nothing wavering. For he that wavereth is like a wave of the sea driven with the wind and tossed. For let not that man think that he shall receive any thing of the Lord. A double minded man is unstable in all his ways.* (James 1:6-8, KJV)

Discord in the Home Hinders Prayer

Finally, discord in the home is a definite hindrance to prayer. Peter specifically mentions this as a hindrance to the prayers of a husband whose attitude toward his wife is less than godly.

Husbands, in the same way be considerate as you live with your wives, and treat them with respect, and as heirs with you of the gracious gift of life, so that nothing will hinder your prayers. (1 Peter 3:7, NIV)

When there is a serious conflict in family relationships and the head of the household is not demonstrating the attitude Peter mentions, the husband's communication with God is hindered. The man who turns away from the truth, lest he should get to know it, will not receive answers to prayer. Likewise, wives are to follow the biblical principle of submission to their husbands' headship or their own prayers to God may be hindered.

> *Scripture: 1 Peter 3:7; Ephesians 5:22-24; James 1:6-7*

Below are other hindrances to a powerful prayer:

- Anxiety and worry (Philippians 4:6)
- Doubt and double-mindedness (James 1:5-8)
- Forsaking God (2 Chronicles 15:2)
- Hypocrisy (Matthew 6:5)
- Lack of humility (2 Chronicles 7:14)
- Failure to honor the wife (1 Peter 3:7)
- Praying amiss or wrong motives (James 4:3-8)
- Pride (Luke 18:10-14)
- Rebellion against God's Word (Zechariah 7:11-14)
- Refusal to hear the truth (Proverbs 28:9)
- Vain (useless) repetitions (Matthew 6:7)
- Willful stubbornness (Jeremiah 16:12-13)

> **Prayer Thought** – *All hindrances to a powerful prayer life can be dealt with at once by coming to God in a prayer of confession and repentance.*
>
> *Scripture: Acts 3:19, James 5:16*

From time to time, we all have issues in our lives that may hinder our prayers. However, we are assured in the Bible of this:

> *If we confess our sins, he is faithful and just to forgive us our sins and to cleanse us from all unrighteousness.* (1 John 1:9, KJV)

Once we confess our sins, we can enjoy a clear and open channel of communication with God. Our prayers will not only be heard and answered, but we will also be filled with a deep sense of joy. Moreover, we will bear much fruit for the kingdom of God.

What Does Hearing God Mean?

Hearing God refers to our readiness to *obey* Him. God does not only speak to give people a chance to decide if they want to obey Him. He also speaks to those who take Him seriously and stand ready to obey and respond according to what He says.

> **Scripture**: *1 John 5:14; 1 Thessalonians 5:16-18; 2 Chronicles 7:14; Isaiah 19:20; John 15:7; Matthew 6:6-7, 33, 10:29; Proverbs 1:24, 28:9; Psalm 66:18-19; Zachariah 7:11-13*

God has promised to hear us if we sincerely approach Him with an attitude to do His will and a willingness to allow His Word to guide and correct us.

> *For the eyes of the Lord are on the righteous, and His ears are open to their prayers; but the face of the Lord is against those who do evil.*
> (1 Peter 3:12, ESV)

God is aware of everything we say and do. Not even a sparrow can fall to the ground without Him knowing it. Therefore, when anyone prays to God, He is well aware of the words that are spoken. Everyone who has a sincere heart, humble spirit, and desire to experience the presence of God (as well as those who seek to establish a personal relationship with Him) should cry out to God, ask Him to forgive them of their sins, and receive Him as Lord and Savior. God will hear their prayers and forgive them of their sins. We know all have sinned and come short of God's glory. However, it is also God's desire that all men are saved. God is no respecter of persons, but He has set an order to be followed. We cannot come to Him any way we feel. We must pray according to His will. Who should pray?

- The one who does not cherish sin in his heart (Psalm 66:18)
- Anyone who does not turn a deaf ear to the law (Proverbs 28:9)
- Those who abide in Christ and Christ's words abide in them (John 15:5)
- He who delights himself in the Lord (Psalm 37:4)
- The oppressed can pray so that God will hear (Psalm 10:18)

A Prayer That God Will Hear

Heavenly Father, we praise You for who You are. You are the great I AM. You are the One who speaks so we can hear Your voice and follow where You lead us.

Lord, we come with our hearts filled with thanksgiving. We give thanks for all You have done for us. We thank You for sending Your Son Jesus to die on Calvary to redeem us from our sins. Thank You for being a forgiving God who looks beyond our faults and sees our needs. We realize we do not deserve it, so we thank You for Your grace and mercy. Thank You, Lord Jesus, for bringing us out of darkness into Your marvelous light. Thank You for giving us our families, loved ones, health, and strength. Lord, thank You for the unconditional and endless love You give us each day. Thank You, Lord, for sending the Holy Spirit to dwell among us, comfort us, and reveal Your Word to us.

Father, today we intercede on behalf of those who do not know You, the ones who are not listening to Your Word, and those who have strayed from the truth.

Prayer Thought – *God speaks to those who take Him seriously and respond to whatever He says. Therefore, let us pray to hear God's voice.*

Scripture: John 10:27, Psalm 85:8

We confess any lack of desire to hear Your voice. Give us ears to hear what Your Spirit is saying to us. Lord, give us listening ears to discern Your voice from the many voices that are speaking.

We petition You, Father God, to open our hearts to the things of God and help us close our ears to the whisperings of the evil one. In Jesus' name, we pray. Amen.

Chapter 2

PRAY FOR THE LOCAL CONGREGATION AND CHURCH LEADERSHIP

Trust in the Lord with all thine heart; and lean not unto thine own understanding. In all thy ways acknowledge him, and he shall direct thy paths.

(Proverbs 3:5-6, KJV)

THE WORK OF THE local congregation (church) is certainly very important, hence, the need for prayer. Yet, sometimes, we lose sight of the fact that there is much work to do. The key is for all of us to start praying more intentionally for our churches and to encourage others to do the same.

The church's prayer for all people is an essential aspect of its participation in the Great Commission. Prayer moves the hand of God. When Paul turns to the matter of instructing the church, he first employs prayer. God commands us to pray for all people, including kings and those who are in authority. Then comes the rationale behind the command: the salvation of all people everywhere is the will of God.

Prayer Points for the Local Congregation

- Pray for a revelation of Jesus Christ, that people might walk in their calling (Ephesians 1:17-19)

- Pray that God will forgive our sins

- Pray that Jesus' presence will be manifested in us, so we may be more intentional in our praying, experience the love of God (Ephesians 3:16-19), and know the will of God for our lives (Colossians 1:9-11)

- Pray for God's love to abound in us resulting in righteous living (Philippians 1:9-11), so we may conduct ourselves in a manner worthy of God (Colossians 1:10)

- Pray for unity in the church that we may dwell together (Ephesians 4:13) and be filled with joy, peace, and hope (confidence) (Romans 15:5-6, 13)

- Pray for a release of grace to bring the church to spiritual maturity, so we may abound in love and holiness (1 Thessalonians 3:10-13), and carry out the Great Commission (Matthew 28:19-20)

Prayer for the Local Congregation

Heavenly Father, we humble ourselves under Your mighty hand. Forgive our sins and cleanse us from all unrighteousness. Let us draw near to You with a true heart in full assurance of faith.

Let Your Word dwell in us richly. Fill us with the knowledge of Your will in all wisdom and spiritual understanding. Being filled will help us live and conduct ourselves in a manner worthy of You, fully pleasing You, being fruitful in every good work and increasing in the knowledge of God (Colossians 1:9-10).

Renew us in the spirit of our minds that we may put on tender mercies, kindness, humility, meekness, and longsuffering bearing with and forgiving one another that we may dwell together in the unity of the faith. May we recognize those who labor among us, esteeming them highly in love for their work's sake.

We pray there are no divisions among us and that we may stand fast in one spirit striving together for the faith. Help us to be more intentional in our prayers. Let us not be tossed about with strange doctrines. Rather, that we study to show ourselves approved unto God and rightly divide the Word of Truth.

Father, forgive us for losing focus and seeking man more than You. Forgive us for our lukewarm ways, complacency, political correctness, and our lack of prayer as a whole.

Help us not to murmur and complain or walk after our own lusts. Let us be rich in good works, ready to give and willing to share. We pray that the whole body will be knit and joined together, and each person will exercise every part and contribute to the growth of the body. As each one has received a gift, let him use it in ministry.

Help us to love one another, look out for the interests of others, and carry out the Great Commission. Let us become serious and watchful in our prayers, redeeming the time, for the days are evil. Allow us to run with endurance the race that is set before us; Help us to set our minds on things above and not on things on the earth. Help us to press toward the mark for the prize of the high calling of Jesus Christ. Let us put on the whole armor of God that we may be able to stand.

Many among us today have special needs in their lives. They need Your unique touch and reassurance right now. Sometimes they don't understand why things happen in their lives but God, allow their faith to look up to You. We pray that their faith will not waiver during these times. Some have family and relationship problems. Bring healing and reconciliation to all members and their families.

Heavenly Father, we need Your guidance and direction. Help us to be faithful over a few things, so that You can make us rulers over many. In Jesus' name, we pray. Amen.

Pray for Effective Leadership

But I would have you know that the head of every man is Christ; and the head of the woman is the man; and the head of Christ is God.

(1 Corinthians 11:3, KJV)

Ministry is time-consuming, and many needs are ever before us. Nevertheless, just as Jesus did, leaders must spend time alone with God to be renewed for the work.

But the news about Him spread even more, and large crowds would come together to hear Him and to be healed of their sicknesses. He often withdrew to deserted places and prayed. (Luke 5:15-16, CSB)

Leaders, including pastors, ministerial staff, officers, as well as department and auxiliary leaders, are gifts to the body of Christ. As a result, they serve on the frontlines of the battle of faith. They need prayer on a consistent basis.

I encourage you to always pray according to God's Word. God is preparing His people for extraordinary work. The only way to do this is through prayer.

If my people, which are called by my name, shall humble themselves, and pray, and seek my face, and turn from their wicked ways; then will I hear from heaven, and will forgive their sin, and will heal their land. (2 Chronicles 7:14, KJV)

Effective Christian leaders are people of sound character who generate trust in their followers. The foundation of Christian character is the believer's union with Jesus Christ. In their death with Christ, believers die to the old self, are raised to a new life with Christ, and are clothed with the character of Christ (Colossians 3:1-17). As the branch receives its life from the vine, so Christians receive their spiritual lives from Christ (John 15:1-17).

Christ, by the power of His Holy Spirit, produces the fruit of the Spirit in the believer—love, joy, peace, patience, kindness, goodness, faithfulness, gentleness, and self-control. The character of Christ in the Christian leader should clearly produce moral excellence, which is crucial to the leader's effectiveness—honesty, integrity, fairness, compassion, service to others, a life of prayer, and total dependence upon God for strength and guidance.

What Is Effective Christian Leadership?

Effective Christian leadership is the process of helping members of the congregation become spiritually mature Christians. Effective Christian leaders model Christ in attitude, behavior, and character (Philippians 2:5; Proverbs 15:13, 17:22; Psalm 51:17).

The Church Has Many Leaders

The New Testament teaches that the task of ministry is shared by all and is not limited to a special, professional class. The ministry of the church is Christ's ministry, shared by all who are in Christ. To understand leadership in the church, you must comprehend a peculiar and mysterious fact about the church: it is the body of Christ. The Bible does not say the church resembles or is like a body. The church *is* the body of Christ (1 Corinthians 12:27). When we think about leadership, we must understand four features of the church as the body of Christ.

1. Christ is the head of the body

The New Testament is clear that Christ is the head of the church. Christ sustains the whole body and supplies what the body needs for life (Colossians 1:18; Ephesians 1:22-23, 4:15-16).

2. The church is a living organism

Christians are members of a living body, not an institution (Ephesians 4:12-16). The source of the church's life is Christ Himself. This implies the church, as a *living organism*, is constantly growing, changing, and adapting to the changing

> **Prayer Thought** – *Peace, harmony, and love are the keys to God's release of His grace to accomplish His work.*
>
> *Scripture: 1 Corinthians 11:18; 1 Timothy 3:5; Acts 14:23; James 5:14; Matthew 18:17*

realities around it. This is what it means to be alive. The word for an organism that has quit growing and changing is *dead.*

3. The church is dependent upon God

Like the vine to the branch, the church is connected to and dependent upon Christ for its very life. As a living organism, the church's concern is not what we want to do, but rather, what Christ is doing in and through us. How is the life of Christ being expressed in our lives as a church?

4. The body of Christ is one with many parts that work together

1 Corinthians 12:12-31 makes it clear that each part of the body is indispensable to the healthy functioning of the entire body. Such mutual interdependence implies mutual accountability that all members of the body of Christ, including leaders, have to Christ and one another.

Prayer Points

- Pray for divine protection of our leaders (2 Corinthians 5:26; Ephesians 6:10-13)

- Pray for the peace of God for our leaders (Colossians 3:15)

- Pray that our leaders walk worthy of their calling and speak the gospel boldly (Colossians 1:9-10; Ephesians 6:19)

- Pray that the leaders will have a deep spiritual passion with fervent love for God and all people (James 5:16)

- Pray that they will weep over the sins of God's people, be sensitive to God's voice, and be led by the Holy Spirit (Ephesians 5:16; Exodus 33:15; John 10:27; Proverbs 14:12)

Prayer for the Church Leadership

Our Father in heaven, we give You praise for leadership. Lord, we praise You as our Shepherd, for You are the one who speaks so we may hear Your voice and follow You where You lead. Give us an ear to hear what the Spirit is saying to the church (Revelation 3:22).

Open our hearts to Your truth. God, we thank You for the men and women of God who give of their time, talent, and treasure to glorify You.

We realize that we are living in perilous times. Men, women, boys, and girls are doing many things that are not according to Your will. Thank You, Lord, for the opportunity to confess our sins to You. Thank You for being a faithful, just, and forgiving God who cleanses us of our sins (1 John 1:9).

We pray that our leader(s) will dwell in the secret place of the Most High and remain stable and fixed under the shadow of the Almighty (Psalm 91:1) whose power no enemy can withstand. Thank You, Jesus, for the angels that encamp around our leaders. Give them the peace of God, which surpasses all understanding in mind, body, and spirit (Philippians 4:7). Give them peace in the midst of their storms. May they prosper and stay in good health even as their souls prosper (3 John 2). We pray that the Spirit of the Lord will rest upon the church as the body of Christ called to intercede through prayer on behalf of others, individually, and collectively.

Fill the leadership with the knowledge of Your will in all wisdom and spiritual understanding (Colossians 1:9-13; Isaiah 11:2). Grant them the joy of having every member of their families saved and healthy. We pray your blessings upon them and their families. Thank You, God, for Jesus who lives to make intercession for us. Even when we don't know what we should pray, we thank You for the Holy Spirit to show us what to pray for our leaders.

Prayer Thought – *Christ is the source of intercessory prayer for the congregation and church leadership.*

Scripture: 1 John 1:9; 1 Timothy 3:1-7; Acts 20:28; Ephesians 4:11-16; Exodus18:21; Hebrews 13:7, 17; James 3:1

We stand in the gap for our leadership that they may continue to walk victoriously in every area (Hebrews 7:25). Bless them financially. Send willing workers who are full of the Holy Spirit to whom Your leaders can delegate specific duties. This will give them more time to pray and study Your Word.

Give the leadership a deep spiritual passion with fervent love for God and His people. Pray that they will observe a personal Sabbath rest and not become burned-out (Matthew 22:37-39; 1 John 4:7-11). Give them boldness, courage, and faith that moves mountains (Hebrews 11:6; Joshua 1:6, 9, 18; Matthew 17:20). In Jesus' name, we pray. Amen.

Chapter 3

PRAY FOR PASTORS, MINISTERS, AND OFFICERS

Take heed therefore unto yourselves, and to all the flock, over the which the Holy Ghost hath made you overseers, to feed the church of God, which he hath purchased with his own blood. (Acts 20:28, KJV)

LOOKING AT THE MINISTRY of Jesus, the New Testament reveals five things Jesus did. These are five keys to true biblical ministry:

1. Jesus built His relationship with His Father

Jesus lived a life of prayer. He started every day in communion with the heavenly Father. He ended every day in close relationship with His Father. At times, He even spent the whole night in communion with His Father. Jesus was actually in touch with His heavenly Father all the time. The first thing He did each day was to fill the well of His being with the presence of His Father.

His ultimate desire was to be in union with the Father and experience the joy of His Sonship. His purpose was to do the will of the Father. He was effective because He received grace and power from the Father. When pastors and ministers adopt prayerful lifestyles as Jesus did and become intentional about discipleship and spiritual formation, God will use them to change the church into a sanctuary for spiritually transformed lives. Jesus said:

It is written, My house shall be called the house of prayer.
(Matthew 21:13, KJV)

Jesus did not say His church should be a place of singing, preaching, or doing ministry. No matter how important these things may be, the church is about leading people to the Lord Jesus Christ where they too can experience the presence of the Lord. Unfortunately, too many technicians have invaded the church with programs and ideas. They have turned it into a human institution rather than the living body of Christ. When each member of the body of Christ lives a life connected with the Heavenly Father, the church becomes a sanctuary of prayer, grace, and the dwelling of the presence of God. Jesus' hunger for the presence of God in His life should be our motivation and inspiration to be more and more like Him.

2. Jesus preached the gospel of the kingdom of God

Jesus often preached, proclaiming a message of God's love. In describing His earthly mission, He said:

> *The Spirit of the Lord is upon me, because he has anointed me to preach the gospel to the poor.* (Luke 4:18, KJV)

> *And Jesus went about all the cities and villages, teaching in their synagogues, and preaching the gospel of the kingdom.* (Matthew 9:35, KJV)

Jesus taught the people every day, giving guidance through His Word, calling them to confess their sins, and to experience transformed lives. The ministry of the Word always will lead people to changed lives. There is power in the *Word.* The *Word* of God brought this world into existence. The *Word* brought Jesus Christ from the grave. The *Word* brings us back to spiritual health and meaningful change.

From an early age, Jesus developed passionate love for the Scriptures. He learned and taught them with *power* and *authority* (Luke 2:46–50). His love for the Father motivated Him to read His Book and learn about His will. Pastors, teachers, and leaders should always lead people to a better understanding of the Word of God.

Notice the following vital spiritual things that the Word does for us:

- God's Word gives us life (Philippians 2:16)
- God's Word can make us righteous (1 Corinthians 15:1-2)
- God's Word can produce growth (1 Peter 2:2)
- God's Word sanctifies us (John 17:7)
- God's Word gives us wisdom (Psalm 119:98)

Jesus did not preach sociology, politics, or psychology. He always preached the Word. For this reason, He had power and authority. Jesus mingled with men as one who desired their good. He showed His sympathy for them, ministered to their needs, won their confidence, and then told them "Follow Me" (Matthew 4:19).

3. Jesus made disciples through the power of the Holy Spirit

As soon as Jesus started His public ministry, He called and empowered twelve men to be His disciples. These twelve men would eventually champion His evangelistic cause. The wisdom of His method of evangelism centered on the fundamental principle of concentrating on those men He intended to use to transform the world.

The harvest is plenteous, but the laborers are few. Theologically speaking, this has always been the methodology of Jesus. He challenged His disciples for this reason by saying,

> *The harvest is plentiful, but the workers are few. Ask the Lord of the harvest, therefore, to send out workers into his harvest field.* (Luke 10:2, KJV)

> *When Jesus saw the crowds, he had compassion on them, because they were harassed and helpless, like sheep without a shepherd.* (Matthew 9:36, NIV)

4. Jesus met the needs of the people

Jesus loves people. He knows they matter to God; therefore, they matter to Him. The first thing He did was to mingle with people, desiring their good. By doing so, He touched their hearts. Secondly, He showed them empathy by meeting them at their daily vocations and showing interest in their secular affairs. Thirdly, He won their confidence. When we build relationships, when needs are met, and hearts are touched, then we invite people to follow Jesus.

Jesus basically says we need more workers and disciples to gather the harvest. So, go and make disciples. Our role is to pray for the harvest and especially for the harvesters.

God's role is to send us people who will be the new harvesters. The need to build disciples is so fundamental that Jesus spent three-and-a-half years in full-time discipleship formation. In fact, if Jesus had not built His disciples, there would not be a church today.

5. Jesus gave His life as a ransom for many

Jesus lived a life of service and sacrifice. Any study of Christian leadership is incomplete unless we study and apply the sacrificial life of Jesus Christ and Him as a servant leader.

There are two important truths about Christ: First, Jesus Christ lived a life of service. Secondly, He was a servant leader.

The Son of Man did not come to be served but to serve. (Mark 10:45, NIV)

I am among you as one who serves. (Luke 22:27, GNT)

The King of the whole universe was not pursuing self-glorification, self-satisfaction, power, or control. He was focused on *service* and *ministry*. Jesus lived a life of sacrifice and gave His life as a living sacrifice to redeem us. Jesus lived, suffered, and died on our behalf. He agonized in Gethsemane, died at Calvary and paid the price for our redemption. In fact, God sent His only Son to die on our behalf. This should give us an idea of just how valuable we are to God. Jesus declared:

The Son of Man came to seek and to save that which was lost.
(Luke 19:10, KJV)

Lost people matter to God. Therefore, to be a genuine pastor and disciple of Jesus Christ, lost people must matter to each believer. The pastor's role is to instill this value in the hearts of each member of the congregation. This sacrificial life manifests itself on at least two levels.

- A life of service giving of your time, resources, and talents
- A life of sacrifice placing others before yourself

God calls us to live as Jesus lived. *Ministry is not about us, but about Him*—knowing and serving Him.

What Must the Pastors and Ministerial Staff Do?

Pastors and ministerial staff must deepen their relationship with the Father through prayer, which results in greater intimacy with Him. Then they will be able to preach the gospel of the kingdom of God and build leaders to take care of the needs of the people. Authentic leadership in the church is about servant leadership. Jesus came to serve, not to be served. He came to offer His life as a sacrifice and service to others. He calls us to do the same.

Prayer Points

- Pray for a powerful anointing on our pastors and ministerial staff. Ask God to reveal Himself to them

- Pray they would have wisdom and understanding in dealing with the challenges of ministry, whether it is physical, emotional, or spiritual

- Pray that the leaders will be faithful and that their faith will not be based on the wisdom of men but the power of God (1 Corinthians 2:5)

- Pray that God will strengthen and bless them and their family relationships, as well as grant them good health

- Pray that God will bring unity among our pastoral and ministerial staff. Ask Him to give the pastoral leadership and ministerial staff vision, guidance, and peace regarding the ministry

Prayer for Pastors and the Ministerial Staff

Father, we thank You that our pastors and the ministerial staff are faithful and You preserve them. Let them abound with blessings and not grow weary in well-doing because You will perfect the good work You have begun in them (Philippians 1:6).

They are Your workmanship created in Christ Jesus and equipped in every good work to do Your will. Do a work in them that is well-pleasing in Your sight. Let all grace abound toward them, having sufficiency in all things and abundance for every good work (2 Corinthians 9:8). Allow them to wait for You. Strengthen them in their hearts. Lord. We lift up our pastors and ministerial staff. Cover them with the blood of Jesus.

Let the fire from the Holy Spirit rest upon every pastor, teacher, evangelist, missionary, prayer intercessor, and leader. Let the spirit of revival come upon the membership to bring forth the move of God and awaken their desires.

Let them be vessels of honor, fit for the Master's use. Allow their speech and preaching to be demonstrations of the Holy Spirit and power. Let them be instant in and out of season to preach the Word.

We pray they will continually triumph in Christ. Teach them the way they should go. Reveal the deeper things of God to them by Your Spirit. Let Your peace rule in their hearts. Help them to operate in the Spirit of God and not conform to the world system. Let them demonstrate a Christ-like attitude of peace and joy in the midst of darkness. In Jesus' name, we pray. Amen.

Pray for the Work of Officers and Staff

Therefore, my dear brothers and sisters, stand firm. Let nothing move you. Always give yourselves fully to the work of the Lord, because you know that your labor in the Lord is not in vain.

(1 Corinthians 15:58, NIV)

Pray for the Work of the Deacons

God uses a specific method to move churches forward. *He calls people to lead* (pastors) and then *He gives the leaders support* (deacons and trustees). They serve the pastor and are fellow servants to the congregation. God also gives leaders the vision for the work of the Lord. The pastor and church board are to *work together in unity* for the advancement of God's kingdom.

What Is a Deacon?

The word *"deacon"* means minister or servant. Deacons were called in the early church to serve tables. The deacons are typically the people in the church who assist the pastor in various duties, from caring for church families to assisting the church's trustees in financial matters. They are called to assist the pastor in the spiritual and moral affairs of the church. This ministry is involved in teaching Bible classes, visiting the sick and shut-in, and serving Communion to those who request it. The deacon's ministry also entails leading prayer meetings and conducting worship services at local nursing homes.

Biblical Qualifications

A person's life and character must pass certain criteria before qualifying to serve in the capacity of a deacon. Hence, the Bible specifies the qualifications of a deacon:

- Not double-tongued (1 Timothy 3:8)

- Not two-faced, deceitful in one's words saying one thing and meaning another, making different representations to various people about the same thing

Prayer Thought – *Christ's method of preaching and teaching through servant leadership and sacrifice builds relationships and meets the needs of people.*

Scripture: 1 Corinthians 2:4, 10-14, 3:6; 2 Corinthians 2:14, 9:8; 2 Timothy 2:21, 4:2; Deuteronomy 8; Ephesians 2:10; Exodus 17:11; Galatians 3:13, 26:9; Hebrews 12:24, 13:21; Isaiah 54:17; Philippians 1:6; Proverbs 28:20; Psalm 27:14, 31:23, 32:8

- Not given to much wine (1 Timothy 3:8)

- Not greedy for money (1 Timothy 3:8)

- Not a person who is eager to gain, especially if such gain degrades his/her moral character

- Proven, tested, and approved (1 Timothy 3:10)

- Blameless (1 Timothy 3:10)

- Not merely unaccusable but unaccused, free from any legal charge

- Good reputation (Acts 6:3)

- Bears honorable testimony, well-testified about, has a good witness

- Husband of one wife (1 Timothy 3:12)—the person must have one wife at a time, not multiple spouses. This does not disqualify those who are not married or who are divorced or widowed

- Rules his children well (1 Timothy 3:12)

- Rules his own house well (1 Timothy 3:12)

- Full of the Holy Spirit (Acts 6:3)

- Full of wisdom (Acts 6:3)—the word "full" means abounding or abundant

Prayer Points

- Pray that deacons are filled with the love of God and have His wisdom

- Pray that deacons walk in honesty and integrity

- Pray that deacons are compassionate and courageous

- Pray that deacons develop strong prayer lives

- Pray that deacons are obedient to the Word of God

Prayer for Deacons

Father God, we praise You for our deacons. You came to serve, not to be served. Create in the deacons a clean heart and renew the right spirit in them. Fill them with Your love that they may love with the love of Christ and share the same love with their fellowmen. Fill their hearts with joy and compassion that they may meet their brothers' needs. Fill them with courage that they may give their lives in service to the church.

Fill them with the power of the Holy Spirit. Make them ministers of Your Word. Transform them by the renewing of their minds. Let them walk worthy before You in honesty and integrity. Help them to put their trust in You. Give them the strength they need. Protect them as they go into the communities ministering to the people. We decree by the power of God that no weapon formed against our deacons shall prosper. In Jesus' name, we pray. Amen.

Pray for the Trustees

Therefore, my beloved brethren, be steadfast, immoveable, always abounding in the work of the Lord, knowing that your labor is not in vain in the Lord. (1 Corinthians 15:58, NKJV)

Pray for the Work of the Trustees

Since the position of trustee is not a biblical office, there are no biblical qualifications provided. However, we believe the biblical qualifications used to select

Prayer Thought – *Christ's method of preaching and teaching through "servant leadership and sacrifice" builds relationships and meets the needs of people.*

Scripture: 1 Corinthians 2:10-14, 3-6, 9:8; 2 Corinthians 2:4, 14-20; 2 Timothy 2:21; Deuteronomy 28; Ephesians 2:10; Exodus 17:11; Galatians 3:13, 6:9; Hebrews 12:24, 13:21; Isaiah 54:17; Philippians 1:6; Psalm 27:14, 31:23, 32:8

deacons should be the same ones used to select trustees. They should all be willing to submit to leadership and willing to regularly attend worship, Bible study, Sunday school, and prayer services.

Trustees are leaders in the church who are responsible for many different things. The decisions trustees make must generally be approved by the entire board of trustees. This board is comprised of a group of several elected trustees and is designed to help the church make wise decisions by taking votes on financial issues. Trustees are state mandated with responsibility for the physical property of the church. They have custodial duties over church property consistent with statutes the state. Trustee boards in churches are frequently granted capacities that are similar to that of a board of deacons. If the board of trustees is granted such capacities, it is recommended that the qualifications be the same as the board of deacons.

God's power is available to us whenever we are willing to become aware of it in our lives. Trustees should put their trust in God.

> *Commit thy works unto the LORD, and thy thoughts shall be established.* (Proverbs 16:3, KJV)

Prayer Points for Trustees

- Set clear mission aims and objectives

- Act responsibly and be accountable

- Act with honesty and integrity

- Be good stewards of church property and funds

- Understand the constitution and make collective decisions

Pray for wisdom as they deal with governance and financial issues and continue to look to the future of our churches. Pray that they will be persons of wisdom with teachable spirits.

Be wise now therefore, O ye kings: be instructed, ye judges of the earth.
Serve the Lord with fear and rejoice with trembling.

(Psalm 2:10-11, KJV)

Prayer for Trustees

Father God, we come to You today in prayer to ask for strength and courage for our trustees as they face multiple challenges in the church. Bless them in a mighty way. Help them to always seek to study Your Word, follow your truth, and minister to all who need Your love and care, particularly the poor, widows, and homeless. Help the trustees to walk in honesty and integrity.

Lord Jesus, let them realize that the authority vested in them is conferred to them, not for themselves but for the service of others. Keep them focused on Your vision and what you have assigned their hands to do.

'When a man's ways are pleasing to the Lord, he makes even his enemies live at peace with him.' (Proverbs 16:7, NKJV)

Give our trustees a strong, trusting relationship with Jesus Christ that they might be good stewards. May Your grace be upon them that they may listen to advice and accept instruction. That way, You can get the glory out of their lives. Give them wisdom and teach them the way of truth as it is seen in Christ. Thus, they can do the work of the ministry and bring glory to Your holy name.

Help them to understand no matter what kind of authority they hold, they share in your ultimate authority, which is a duty of love and service. Enable them to act on this knowledge and to serve in a sacrificial manner. In the name of Jesus. Amen.

Prayer Thought – *Trust in the Lord who created you and He will forever sustain you.*

Scripture: Jeremiah 17:7-8; Proverbs 3:5, 16:3

Pray for the Work of the Church Administration

Church administration is a spiritual service to the body of Christ. It involves the wise stewardship of God's resources for the accomplishment of the work of the ministry. Church administration or management has to do with the organization of church ministry and the operations that govern that organization. Administration is not an *end* of itself. However, it is a *means* for serving people effectively while making efficient use of resources in a manner that glorifies God.

These management goals are served by having biblically consistent policies and procedures in writing and available for reference. These policies and procedures give direction and definition to the "how" of ministry. Those who manage ministry are given significant trust. God is honored and believers are encouraged when church affairs are administered well. Therefore, church administrators should be spiritually mature and able to work well with others. Also, they should be able to plan, organize, oversee, and evaluate ministry wisely according to biblical principles.

Prayer Points

- Pray that the church administrators will ensure all church matters are handled effectively with the goals of biblical ministry clearly in view

- Pray that they reduce the possibility of mismanagement and unethical behavior, particularly in matters pertaining to personnel and finances

- Pray that they save time in the decision-making process, enabling the ministry to function more efficiently

- Pray that they clarify expectations and enable people to work together in ministry with a greater understanding

- Pray that they will develop in their prayer lives

Prayer for the Church Administrators

Heavenly Father, we thank You for our church administrators. Thank You for Your Holy Spirit, which empowers and enables the smooth running of your church on daily basis. Give vision, wisdom, good judgment, and courage to the administrative pastor, business manager, and the staff. Increase their faith to believe You for the impossible. Help them to remember that You provide the power for them to administer and the work they do is Your work. Give them joy as they work together to carry out the work of the ministry. Let them not be discouraged when things don't go their way. We thank You for placing them in the body as it pleased You. May the work they do be a blessing to the body of Christ.

Help the administrative staff to avoid controversies, dissensions, and quarrels over those things that are unprofitable. Let their lives be a witness of You. We confess that sometimes it is not easy to love the unlovable. Fill the administrators with Your Spirit that they may put on the love of Christ. When they become frustrated and impatient, encourage their hearts.

We thank You for every volunteer. We pray that You will grace them with Your presence. Help them to be confident that the Greater One is on the inside of them.

'He who has done a good work in them will perform it until the day of Jesus Christ' (Philippians 1:6). In Jesus' name, we pray. Amen.

Prayer Thought – *In humility, may the work they do be a blessing to the body of Christ.*

Scripture: 1 Corinthians 15:58

The Pastor's Priority

by Rev. Dr. Adron Robinson

Prayer and preaching are the pastor's priority. You must discipline your time to allow for prayer and the ministry of the Word. If you are not intentional about spending time with God and His Word, you will find yourself giving God your leftovers instead of your first fruit. It takes time to pray and it takes time to study and craft biblically sound sermons. So, set aside the hours to do what God called you to do and delegate the things that others can do. Every Christian can serve, but the pastor is called to preach the Word.

> But we will devote ourselves to prayer and to the ministry of the word. (Acts 6:4, ESV)

There are 168 hours in a week, and most weeks seem to go by way too fast. Each week has a variety of good things you can do to fill those hours: community meetings, phone calls, pastoral care, staff development, membership concerns, teaching, sermon preparation, and the list goes on. But how do you determine how much time to spend on each of them when there are so many options?

In Acts 6:1-4, the church was growing rapidly, and because of this, the disciples had to make some hard decisions about how to divide their time. There were people in need and ministry to be done, and they had the same 168 hours a week that you and I have. But they made a decision to prioritize their time by focusing on what God called them to do and to delegate to capable people that which was not their calling.

The apostles said: "It is not right that we should give up preaching the Word of God to serve tables." And pastor, it is not right for you to serve tables at the neglect of prayer and preaching the gospel.

Prayer Prompt

Lord, Sundays seem to come so fast and there is so much work to do. Grant us your wisdom and discernment to make prayer and preaching our first priority, so that we can commit our time to our calling.

[© Rev. Dr. Adron Robinson, Pastor of Hillcrest Baptist Church in Country Club Hills, Illinois IBSA President. Used by permission]

Chapter 4

PRAY FOR DEPARTMENT AND AUXILIARY LEADERS

From whom the whole body, joined and held together by every joint with which it is equipped, when each part is working properly, makes the body grow so that it builds itself up in love. (Ephesians 4:16, ESV)

DEPARTMENT LEADERS FACILITATE AN effective Bible-based learning strategy for Sunday and Bible school.

Organization: This involves grouping for departments/divisions and classes based on a proper teacher to student ratio.

Delegation: This involves building teams to assist and delegate responsibilities to. In addition to having teachers, helpers, and department heads, superintendents benefit by also having assistants and/or secretaries to help them with various details. While all these tasks can be delegated, superintendents still need to supervise those to whom tasks are assigned. They must give deadlines, as well as a means of reporting and accountability.

Staffing: This involves the recruitment of teachers, providing training to equip and encourage them, etc. Staff meetings must be held to get them involved in the planning process, to keep them informed, and build an atmosphere of teamwork.

Coordination: This involves scheduling, facility/room usage based on group sizes and age-level developmental space needs, dealing with safety/security issues, allocating and/or managing budget needs, etc.

Planning: This involves strategizing the best way to accomplish various tasks that need to be done annually, quarterly, or weekly. It also includes developing a planning calendar for the various tasks to be accomplished.

Promotion: This involves working together with the Christian Education Department, which includes Vacation Bible School, Sunday School, and Bible School.

Most importantly, seek God through prayer and the study of His Word. He will give you wisdom and understanding as you look to Him.

Great Leaders are Good Followers

Great leaders are as equally in tune with how to follow well as they are with how to lead well. A few thoughts on good followers are listed below.

- Good followers are finishers. They get the job done, take projects across the finish line, and make things happen on their own

- Good followers anticipate. They understand what needs to be done next before having to be told and are always looking for ways to make the process better

- Good followers criticize in private and praise in public. Praising others in public helps edify and build up the body rather than tear it down

- Good followers are trustworthy. When given an assignment, a leader can be assured it will get done by the followers. They model dependability which is incredibly important

- Good followers will embrace the vision. They take on, embody, and live out the vision and mission of their leaders and the organization, helping set and model a cultural standard

- Good followers make their leaders better. They push their leaders and know how to "lead up" appropriately and intentionally

- Good followers exemplify the characteristics of leadership. They don't need to be managed. They are self-aware and do not need all the attention from the leader

- Good followers are disciplined. They are humble, disciplined, and have complete integrity. They know it is not about them and what you see is what you get

Prayer Points

Pray that department leaders will...
- Spend more time in the Word of God and in prayer
- Have a sincere passion for their ministry
- Be obedient and committed to the things of God and build each other up
- Seek godly wisdom, counsel, and be a good follower
- Walk in humility and in the spirit of love

Prayer for the Department Leaders

Heavenly Father, we thank You for blessing our church with department leaders. We lift them up to You right now. Help us to respect and honor them as they direct the affairs of the church. May they wholeheartedly give their attention to prayer and the ministry of the Word. Grant them gentleness and honesty as they deal with the people (1 Timothy 3:1-2, 5:17; Acts 6:4; Titus 1:7).

May their love for You and one another prove they are your disciples.

Give them a spirit of unity so they may glorify You. Help them see others as You see them. Use them as Your servants to rescue people from darkness and bring them into Your marvelous light. We pray that the favor of the Lord, the authority of the Lord, and the harvest of the Lord will rest upon our department leaders. Teach them to do their part in serving, giving, teaching, or any other area where there is a need.

Protect them from the attacks of the evil one. We bind the evil forces of rebellion, seduction, and pride from attacking our church, and we loose our leaders. In Jesus' name. We cast down vain imaginations and every high thing that exalts itself against the knowledge of God, never more to rise and destroy (2 Corinthians 10:5). We declare they are under our feet. In Jesus' name.

Father, we thank You that no weapons formed against our department leaders will prosper. We pray that Your presence and peace will keep them, and they will dwell in the secret place of the Most High God. Deliver them from terror, fiery darts, doubt, sickness, and diseases (Psalm 91:5, 6). We thank You, Lord God, for encamping Your angels all around them and keeping them in all of their ways (Psalm 91:11).

Lord, let our department leaders have discerning spirits. Renew their strength by the power of the Holy Spirit. Let them wait upon You and mount up with wings as eagles. May they run but not be weary, walk and not faint (Isaiah 40:27-31). In Jesus' name, we pray. Amen.

You can't be a good follower unless you follow the example of Christ. Jesus is the greatest leader because He is the greatest follower. He followed His Father perfectly in all things. The world teaches that leaders must be mighty; however, the Lord teaches that they must be meek. Worldly leaders gain power and influence through their talents, skills, and wealth, but it is only temporary. Spiritual leaders receive power from the Holy Spirit, which is eternal.

Pray for the Auxiliary Leaders

True authority will always put God at the center of its influence through obedience to Him. Many human leaders like King Saul fell from grace because of disobedience as he sought his own power and influence through worldly wisdom.

It is the unity of staff working together that gives spiritual leaders the support they need to lead. But it is all wrapped up in the individual being surrendered to God's will.

God equips His people for every good work (2 Timothy 3:16-17); that should say something about the importance of godly leaders. The point is that *leaders* should *lead.* Church leaders influence others by their godly examples and teaching God's Word (Hebrews 13:7).

Leadership requires having a clear biblical picture of what the local church ought to be and do. Auxiliary leaders have a responsibility to walk with God. They must be careful to maintain good character before God and others (2 Timothy 3:13-18).

The New Testament clearly teaches that leadership in the local church is to be *plural* (Acts 14:23; 20:17; Titus 1:5). *Plural leadership* will *safeguard against the abuse of authority.* Auxiliary leaders are called to *work together.* They focus on building relationships. The entire Bible is summed up by the two great commandments, which are both relational: *love God* and *love others.* This means that church leaders must work at relating to one another in love and help church members relate to one another in love.

The church is not to be run as a business where we make plans and implement those plans according to the best of human wisdom. *The church is to move forward by faith in the living God* and by dependence on Him through prayer. Our aim for auxiliary leaders is to seek the mind of Christ for His church as we wait upon Him through *prayer* and *faith.*

Prayer Points

- Pray that auxiliary leaders are led by the Holy Spirit, and their faith does not stand in the wisdom of men, but in the power of God

Prayer Thought – *If you want to be a great leader, you must first become a good follower.*

Scripture: Mark 10:43-45

- Pray for boldness and a heart filled with compassion as they interact with and serve others

- Pray for grace and wisdom to be encouragers to the body of Christ with love, patience, humility, and to develop in their relationship with God

- Pray that they walk blameless before God, bring peace and joy, and become men and women after God's own heart

- Pray that they will be clothed in the righteousness of Christ, that they may be able to live holy lives

Prayer for the Auxiliary Leaders

Eternal God, we come before Your holy throne interceding on behalf of the auxiliary leaders. Give them a deeper understanding of You and their role as leaders. We pray, Heavenly Father, that they will be led by Your Holy Spirit, which will lead them into all truth. Grow our leaders to be more like You, Jesus. Help them to see You as their greatest treasure. Help them to willingly submit to Your authority in obedience to Your will.

Help them to grow in grace and in the knowledge of You, Lord God. Give them godly wisdom, boldness to persevere, and strength to carry out the vision You have assigned to their hands. We ask that all auxiliary leaders would trust in the Lord with all their hearts and lean not to their own understanding (Proverbs 3:5-6).

Father, cover the auxiliary leaders with the blood of Jesus. You have given Your angels charge over them to keep them wherever they go (Psalm 91:11). Help them develop in their prayer lives and increase their study of the Word of God. Give them the strength as they interact with others.

We pray that each auxiliary leader will put on the whole armor of God, so they may be able to stand in the evil day.

We ask that they will stand their ground, putting on the sturdy belt of truth and the body armor of God's righteousness. For shoes, we pray they will put on the peace that comes from the Good News, so they will be fully prepared. Arm them with faith as their shield to stop the fiery arrows of the enemy. May they put on the helmet of salvation and take the sword of the Spirit, which is the Word of God (Ephesians 6:17). In Jesus' name, we pray. Amen.

Brad Lomenick said, "Good followers are finishers. They get the job done, take projects across the finish line and make things happen on their own." The more you grow in your relationship with God, the bolder your prayers can become because now, your heart will begin to line up with God's heart.

Prayer Thought – *Great leaders are equally in tune with how to follow well as how to lead well.*

Scripture: John 13:13-17

Chapter 5

GLOBAL PRAYER

> *But you will receive power when the Holy Spirit comes on you; and you will be my witnesses in Jerusalem, and in all Judea and Samaria, and to the ends of the earth. (Acts 1:8, BSB)*

PRAYER IS OUR MOST powerful tool in global missions, and it is the key to maintaining a godly perspective. Before we engage in relationships, service, and gospel proclamation, we must first continue to engage in spiritual battles through prayer.

People all over the world are hungry to hear about the saving grace of Jesus Christ. It is our mission to share that good news. We should encourage missionaries, church planters, and leaders to go on the mission field with a passion for fulfilling the Great Commission as given in the following scripture.

> *Go ye therefore, and teach all nations, baptizing them in the name of the Father, and of the Son, and of the Holy Ghost: Teaching them to observe all things whatsoever I have commanded you: and lo, I am with you always, even unto the end of the world.*
>
> (Matthew 28:19-20, KJV)

Prayer Points for Global Missions

- Pray for the accomplishment of the Great Commission: for disciples to be made, churches to be multiplied, and Christ to be magnified in every nation

- Pray for a movement of disciple-makers that will spread the gospel from neighborhoods and workplaces in the city to neighborhoods and workplaces among the nations (Matthew 28:19-20)

- Pray for the missionaries you know who have been sent out from the local church to serve Christ around the world. Then pray that God would raise up and send out more missionaries from our local churches to go into the world's unreached people groups (Matthew 9:35-38)

- Pray that our missionaries would have a heart for lost souls and a passion for missions.

- Pray for wisdom in the development and implementation of church planters and partnerships (Romans 1:8-15). Specifically, pray for this same wisdom and courage in one another's lives as each team leads the local church for the sake of global mission (Acts 6:5-8)

Prayer for Global Missions

Father God, move upon the hearts of Your people to pray for Your saving grace among the nations. Burden the hearts of missionaries and intercessors with people who have no access to the gospel. Help them to pray Bible-filled prayers around the globe. Do not let them lose sight of the one lost sheep nearby but give them a passion for Your worldwide call to do missions. May they feed Your sheep from every part of the earth.

Give them hearts filled with compassion for lost souls as they go out and tell others about Jesus. May they witness to the poor, alcoholics, drug addicts, gamblers, prostitutes, the despised and the outcast, and tell them about Jesus. We pray that many souls will be saved. May they be touched by the Holy Spirit and empowered to overcome their addictions.

We move with the expectation that great things will be done in Jerusalem, Judea, Samaria, and the ends of the earth. We pray that we can reach across cultural and social barriers within new communities of faith throughout the globe. Let there be an awakening in the churches all over the world where those who are lost will come running wanting to know what they must do to be saved.

Holy Spirit, we welcome You in this place. It is through Your transformational work that we lift up the name of Jesus in the four corners of the earth. We pray that the hearts of God's people are made one. May we submit ourselves to You, Lord God, so You will get the glory out of our lives. In Jesus' name, we pray. Amen.

Pray for the Government Leaders

Right relationships are essential for effective praying. We come to God through Jesus Christ in repentance, in continual humility and submission to the King of kings and Lord of lords, and in right relationships with one another. Jesus emphasizes having right relationships in the context of answered prayers (Mark 11:25; Matthew 6:14, 18). The first principle of a right relationship is forgiveness. Jesus said when you stand praying, you must first forgive (Mark 11:25).

There is an attitude that is corrupting to our nation and government leaders: self-righteous arrogance. It has caused many Christians to tear apart the godly fabric of our nation.

God wants to make a shift so that the churches can fully become a powerful force for God's purpose in this generation and those to come. We are the salt of the earth. Paul is instructing Timothy in his letter. It is *we*, not *they* that have sinned. We are responsible for the state of our nation, not sinners. Scripture teaches that the church is the salt of the earth. When the salt loses its savor, ungodly men trample it (Matthew 5:13).

Prayer Thought – *Prayer is our most powerful tool to assist us in taking the gospel of Jesus Christ to the ends of the earth.*

Scripture: Acts 1:8

Prayer Points for the Government

- Pray for an awakening among Christians to have a greater understanding of the time and to seize the day to shine for Jesus. Ask God to give them strategies on how to equip the next generation

- Pray for God to raise up leaders in government who will stand for what is right, so they would be willing to seek God's guidance and wisdom in decision making. In doing so, they will uphold a standard of righteous values for our nation

- Pray that God will open the hearts of leaders to hear and respond to the gospel message if they do not know Him (Acts 16:14)

- Pray for divine protection (Psalm 91) and the peace of Jerusalem

- Pray that God will give them vision, understanding of His Word, and that the Holy Spirit would come upon them, so they may do the work of the ministry

Prayer for the Government

Father, we bring the needs of our government before You and ask You to bless our nation through godly leaders. We magnify the name of Jesus and declare You are Lord over our government.

'I exhort therefore, that, first of all, supplications, prayers, intercessions, and giving of thanks, be made for all men; For kings, and for all that are in authority; that we may lead a quiet and peaceable life in all godliness and honesty. For this is good and acceptable in the sight of God our Savior.' (1 Timothy 2:1-3, KJV)

We pray, in the name of the Lord Jesus Christ, for our president, vice president, all the cabinet, and the justices of the Supreme Court. May they receive the wisdom of God to act in obedience to godly wisdom and for the power of God to flow in their lives. We pray for the members of the Senate and the House of Representatives to find Your peace and direction. May they act and lead according to Your Word. Scripture says that a house divided against itself cannot stand (Mark 3:25). Therefore, we pray for them to be unified in righteousness.

We pray for divine protection to cover all of our law enforcement officers and the men and women of the military. We ask for godly counsel and wisdom for judges across this land, in the name of Jesus. We pray that You and Your kingdom of righteousness will manifest in the hearts of all those who are in authority.

Father, Your Word says to pray for the peace of Jerusalem because those who love Jerusalem shall prosper. You love Jerusalem, and we pray it will receive the peace of God, which brings wholeness. We pray that no leader of our nation will make any decision to harm Jerusalem in any way.

Reveal Your perfect will to all the leaders of Israel. Pour out Your Spirit upon our government leaders and make Your Word known to them. Deliver them from the way of evil and evil men. Make their hearts and ears attentive to godly counsel by doing what is right.

'Love and faithfulness keep a king safe; through love his throne is made secure.' (Proverbs 20:27, NIV)

We decree by the power of God that no weapon formed against our government shall prosper. In Jesus' name, we pray. Amen.

Prayer Thought – *Government leaders should have a deep and abiding faith in God, the wisdom to protect the interest of the people, and uphold the laws of the land.*

Scripture: 1 Chronicles 20:32; 1 Timothy 2:1-3; Hebrews 12:27; John 5:14-15; Mark 3:25; Proverbs 1:23, 2:10-12, 8:15-16, 17:7; Proverbs 20:26, 21:1, 28:2-4, 29:4; Psalm 1:1-2, 25:21, 122:6.

Pray for the Nations

And seek the peace of the city whither I have caused you to be carried away captives and pray unto the Lord for it: for in the peace thereof shall ye have peace. (Jeremiah 29:7, KJV)

This was the Lord's instruction to the children of Israel when they were captives in the city of Babylon. As Christians, this Scripture verse also emphasizes the relevance of our journey in the nation where we live. We may not be in captivity like Babylon, but we are enslaved by sin.

We all want to move through our streets safely. We want to feel secure as we commute. We want law and order without abuse of human rights. We want a cleaner environment. So, we must pray!

The apostle Paul stood up in front of a group of philosophers in a pagan city and preached an amazing message found in Acts 17:26. You were chosen and appointed to live in a particular time and place; the boundaries of the nation were set before the beginning of time in order that man might seek and find the Lord! Our attitudes and involvement as intercessors and Spirit-filled Christians in the nation play a major part in our own spiritual destinies and inheritances.

Later, as Paul is about to give up his life for the gospel, he writes instructions to Timothy, his spiritual son, new apostle, and elder in the church. Prayer is the first assignment to the church when it comes together. Paul is letting Timothy know what the church must do when it comes together (1 Timothy 2:1). It is no different in our day.

Prayer Points for the Nations

- Pray that God will raise a standard in this nation, that the glory of the Lord will be revealed, and we will return to God

- Ask God to grant them wisdom and the ability as nations to pursue peace. May He cause them to build up one another as nations and not tear each other down.

- Pray that God will grant them the ability to walk in love toward all men and see beyond racial, ethnic, and cultural differences

- Pray for spiritual renewal. Ask God to send laborers into the vineyard to share the good news to the poor in spirit, heal the brokenhearted, deliver the captives, bring recovery of sight to the blind, and set at liberty them that are bruised

- Pray that God will grant our leaders the grace to live and conduct themselves honorably and becomingly as in the day, not in revelling and drunkenness, immorality, debauchery, quarrelling, and jealousy

Prayer for the Nations

Father, awaken the nations! Let the earth hear the voice of the Lord. The whole creation groans to be delivered from the bondage of corruption, into the glorious liberty of the children of God. Send forth Your Holy Spirit to bear witness of You and convict the world of sin. Cause Your people to repent, pray, and turn from their wicked ways. You said it is only then that You will hear, forgive, and heal (2 Chronicles 7:14). Shake the nations, so they will come to know You as their Lord and Savior.

Father, cause Your people to rise up. Bring the multitudes into the valley of decision. Send Your ambassadors into all the nations. Open doors for the gospel of the kingdom to be preached to all the world.

We also pray for our nation, the United States of America. May we be beacons of light in this dark world so none may stumble because of us. We pray that every unsaved soul may receive salvation. Lord, open the eyes of the ones who do not know You. Cause the scales to fall from their eyes that they may see the power of God. Give wisdom to our leaders so they may make the right decisions. You said in Your Word that blessed is the nation whose God is the Lord (Psalm 33:12).

May this be a new era for America as we humble ourselves and acknowledge You alone as our Lord and Savior. Give wisdom to our president, vice president, cabinet members, and the men and women in Congress.

We pray for our military personnel stationed around the world. We know the dangers they face day after day. Cover them with the blood of Jesus. Encamp Your angels all around them. Keep them from all hurt, harm, and danger. We decree no weapon formed against them shall prosper. In Jesus' mighty name. Amen.

Pray for the World Leaders

Where there is no vision, the people perish: but he that keepeth the law, happy is he. (Proverbs 29:18, KJV)

Prayer Points

- Pray that all leaders will be in unity and attuned to the Holy Spirit for direction

- Pray for leaders to speak the Word with boldness wherever they go

- Pray for leaders to pursue righteousness, faith, love, and peace

- Pray for discernment between God's wisdom and human wisdom

- Pray for clear vision for world leaders

Prayer for World Leaders

Our Father and our God, we praise You for Your goodness to our nation. You give us blessings we do not deserve. America has turned her back on You. Help us, as a nation, to turn back to You in repentance and faith. Set our feet on the path of Your righteousness and peace. We pray today for our nation's leaders. Give them the wisdom to know what is right and the courage to do the right thing. May this be a new era for America as we humble ourselves and acknowledge You alone as our Lord and Savior.

Father God, Your Word tells us to pray for all the leaders in the nations and those who are in authority over us. So we come to You on their behalf. We pray for Your guidance as they continue to assume the responsibilities of the office they have been chosen to lead. May You bring clarity to their vision and grant strategies that they may skillfully execute their mandates.

'There is a way that seems right to man, but the end thereof are the ways of death.' (Proverbs 16:25, KJV)

We pray for Your grace, mercy, forgiveness, and restoration for each leader. We pray for our president and his cabinet; wipe out greed, corruption, scheming, wicked devices, dishonesty, vain imaginations, evil thoughts, and illegal, underhanded activities from among them. Let them lead in righteousness, truth, and integrity.

Raise up godly men and women with the knowledge and understanding of Your Word who seek after Your heart and who will uphold Your laws and statutes. We pray for all those in authority. Give them wisdom and discernment as they lead. Send strong, faithful men and women to serve this nation and Your people.

Surround them with strong spiritual support and godly people who will encourage them in the work they do. Help them to do good and not evil, to love You first with all their hearts, souls, might, and strength and to love others as they love themselves.

Help them to point people in the right direction so they can lift the standard of morality. Enable them to lead people into a closer relationship with the living God, so the United States of America will once again become a nation that loves the Lord.

Prayer Thought – *Prayer and action are the keys to establish change in the future.*

Scripture: 2 Chronicles 7:14; Haggai 2:7; Joel 3:12-13; Psalm 33:12

We confess that as a nation, we have been rebellious and made light of Your laws. Forgive us for shutting You out of our lives.

Let Your Word go forth as a two-edged sword piercing through the darkness, destroying satanic weapons, and tearing down every stronghold of the enemy. Root out all forms of evil and allow Your Word to heal the sick, comfort and strengthen the weak, give hope to the hopeless, and restore faith in Your leaders that they will believe You for the impossible. We pray for the families of our leaders. Cover them with the blood of Jesus. Put a hedge of protection around them. In Jesus' name, we pray. Amen.

The Anointing of the Holy Spirit

In our culture today, we find that many church people are only concerned about themselves and their own problems. When they talk to others, their conversation is more about everybody's business than it is about petitioning God. However, in Acts 12:5, we see the early church praying without ceasing.

Great power and deliverance are found in prayer. The Bible is full of people who prayed.

- Moses prayed and God spared Israel from judgment
- Joshua prayed and God caused the sun to stand still
- Hannah prayed and God gave her a baby boy
- Solomon prayed and God gave him wisdom
- Elijah prayed and God sent fire down from heaven
- Jonah prayed and God brought him out of the belly of the whale
- The thief on the cross prayed and God gave him eternal life

The Importance of Prayer in the Life of the Believer

Prayer is the very essence of Christianity. It was the only thing Christ's disciples ever asked Him to teach them (Luke 11:1-4). Prayer is to be the heart of the church. Jesus declared:

My house will be called a house of prayer. (Matthew 21:13, KJV)

Arnold Cook suggests that the following test will show how effective we are at leading from our knees:

- Personal Life: How important would your children consider prayer to be based on what they see in your private and family prayer life?

- Marriage: Would your spouse describe your leadership as leading from your knees?

- Professional Life: Is your prayer life commensurate with your sphere of ministry responsibility?

- Leadership: How would your staff rate the importance of prayer in ministry based on what they see in your leadership?

Leadership prayerlessness is sin. The prophet Samuel considered it to be a sin not to pray for the people he was leading.

> *Moreover as for me, God forbid that I should sin against the Lord in ceasing to pray for you: but I will teach you the good and the right way.* (1 Samuel 12:23, KJV)

What If Preachers Pray?

When preachers pray, they depend on God. However, when they do not, they depend on themselves rather than God.

> *Trust in the Lord with all your heart and do not lean on your own understanding.* (Proverbs 3:5, ESV)

What If Leaders Pray?

When leaders pray, they are declaring absolute dependence on the Lord and are walking by faith in God alone, not by sight. When leaders pray, they put God first!

Prayer Thought – *Leadership is not about being known; it is about being known for making a difference.*

Scripture: Proverbs 16:12, Psalm 78:22

*But seek ye first the kingdom of God, and his righteousness; and all
these things shall be added unto you.* (Matthew 6:33, KJV)

When leaders pray, they are unified. As leaders reaffirm the supremacy of Christ
by embracing the whole gospel message, unity and disciple-making will increase
and progress will be made toward our goal of reaching the future generations.

What If the Church Prays?

When the church goes to its knees in prayer, the presence of God is perceived.
Suddenly, we know He is with us working, moving, and answering our prayers.

You may ask if God is not always present when two or three are gathered
together in Christ's name. Yes, but we do not always recognize God's presence.
Jacob said of Bethel:

> *Surely the Lord is in this place and I was not aware of it.*
>
> (Genesis 28:16, NIV)

The church *must* come together in *unity*. It was not only the apostles who prayed
in the upper room. They all prayed. Here was a group of believers concerned
enough to gather in one place for one purpose—to pray. This is a testimony of
the power of united prayer. They were all with one accord in one place (Acts 2:1).

Not only were they all there praying, but they were also all praying for the same
purpose. That is the kind of praying that shakes the place. When God's people come
together with one heart, the presence of God is manifested. When the church prays,
the power of God is received. And they were all filled with the Holy Ghost.

Upon the conclusion of their prayers, the Spirit of God filled every believer
gathered in that room. They were *all* filled, not just the apostles, but every
member of the church. There was a filling on the Day of Pentecost (Acts 2:1-4).
The church cannot operate on past experiences. The church's experience of God
must always be fresh. Every new task demands a new filling. The point of their
prayer was to give them boldness to continue speaking the Word, so Jesus would
be glorified. That was what God called them to do in the first place.

Now, let us put it all together. The disciples' prayers brought a fresh supply of the power of God. They acknowledged God to be their Sovereign Lord and submitted to Him and His redemptive purpose. Any Christian who recognizes and submits to the Lordship of Jesus Christ will be filled with the anointing of the Holy Spirit. When the church prays, the purpose of God is achieved.

And they spoke the word of God with boldness. (Acts 4:31, KJV)

When a church is filled with the Spirit of God, the people will speak the Word of God with boldness. You cannot divorce the Holy Spirit from witnessing. The power of God is given to accomplish the purpose of God. Unless we are willing to be instruments of His purpose, it is useless to pray for His power. Witnesses aren't made by training programs. Such programs are good and may teach a man how to witness, but they will not make him a witness. Only the anointing of the Holy Spirit can do that.

What Does the Anointing of the Holy Spirit Mean?

The anointing is the manifest presence of God. The word "anointing" means "to rub with oil, especially in order to consecrate something (holy object) or someone (holy person)." The anointing is tangible and when God manifests His presence, something supernatural happens. The anointing supernaturally equips us to perform supernatural things. God's anointed vessels are clothed with the mantle of God's supernatural power. God anoints people who love Him more than they love their own lives and love others as themselves. As we open our hearts to love others, God's anointing flows through us. When we close our hearts to others, we grieve the Holy Spirit.

But whoever has this world's goods, and sees his brother in need, and shuts up his heart from him, how does the love of God abide in him? (1 John 3:17, KJV)

Keep your heart with all diligence, for out of it are the issues of life.

(Proverbs 4:23, KJV)

The anointing of the Holy Spirit is given through people to demonstrate God's love and power. Christ means the "Anointed One." Because Christ is in us, we have the same anointing He had on the earth.

> *The Spirit of the Lord is upon Me, because He has anointed Me To preach the Gospel to the poor; He has sent Me to heal the broken-hearted, to proclaim liberty to the captives, recovery of sight to the blind, to set at liberty those who are oppressed; To proclaim the acceptable year of the Lord.* (Luke 4:18-19, KJV)

Some Christians have this anointing while others do not. The anointing is given to preach the gospel to the poor and to bring the revelation of God's love to those who are seeking it. It is given to heal and restore people, proclaim freedom to the captives, open blind eyes, and set people free. The anointing flows and proclaims in God's timing.

The Holy Spirit's Connection to Prayer

When our prayer lives are filled with the Holy Spirit, it takes on a whole new dimension. Let's look at some ways the Holy Spirit is connected to prayer.

Prayer is one of the most powerful weapons a Christian can have. Yet, many believers find it to be a difficult practice.

Several times in the Bible, the Holy Spirit moved upon people in the context of prayer. When the early church was waiting for the first outpouring of the Holy Spirit, Scripture says they continued with one accord in prayer and supplication (Acts 1:14). They were not just waiting passively; they were praying passionately. Then they were filled with the Spirit.

> *And when they had prayed, the place where they were assembled together was shaken; and they were all filled with the Holy Spirit, and they spoke the word of God with boldness.* (Acts 4:31, KJV)

The church was experiencing persecution, and so they came together to pray. As a result, they were filled with the Holy Spirit and had a fresh boldness to declare

God's Word.

Even in the case of Jesus' anointing with the Spirit for His ministry, there is a connection to prayer.

When all the people were being baptized, Jesus was baptized too; And as he was praying, heaven was opened and the Holy Spirit descended on him in bodily form upon him like a dove. (Luke 3:21-22, NIV)

Let us not forget that Jesus was praying when the Holy Spirit came upon Him. Prayer ushers in the presence of the Holy Spirit. To be a Spirit-filled believer, you must be a praying believer. To be a Spirit-filled church, you must be a praying church.

The Holy Spirit Empowers Us to Pray

Not only is the Holy Spirit connected to prayer, but He also empowers us to pray.

Likewise, the Spirit also helps in our weaknesses. For we do not know what we should pray for as we ought, but the Spirit Himself makes intercession for us with groanings which cannot be uttered. Now He who searches the hearts knows what the mind of the Spirit is, because He makes intercession for the saints according to the will of God.

(Romans 8:26-27, NKJV)

Prayer Thought – *Praying the Word of God by faith yields much fruit of the Spirit.*

Scripture: 1 Corinthians 12:7-10, 13:8-10, 14:37; 1 John 5:14-15; 1 Kings 8:33-36, 46-53; 1 Timothy 2:1-8, 3:16-17; 2 Chronicles 7:14, 33:10-13; Colossians 3:17; Daniel 9:3-12; Ephesians 5:20; Genesis 18:27; Hebrews 4:14-16; James 1:5-8, 4:3, 5:16; John 14:13-14, 15:16, 16:23-24, 26; Luke 18:9-14; Matthew 6:9-10, 26:3; Mark 11:24, 16:16; Psalm 32:5-7; Romans 1:8

Chapter 6

PRAYER AND FASTING

> *The powerhouse for the church is not the boardroom but the prayer room.*
> —*Rev. Harry Scism*

I T IS OFTEN SAID that the leader who lasts is the leader who fasts. The leader who stays is the leader who prays.

Definition of Prayer and Fasting

"Prayer and fasting" is defined as voluntarily going without food to focus on prayer and fellowship with God. Prayer and fasting often go hand-in-hand, but this is not always the case. You can pray without fasting and fast without prayer. When these two activities are combined and dedicated to God's glory, they reach their full effectiveness. Having a dedicated time of prayer and fasting is not a way of manipulating God into doing what you desire. Rather, it is simply forcing yourself to focus and rely on God for the strength, provision, and wisdom you need.

The theology of fasting is one of priorities in which believers are given the opportunity to express themselves in undivided and intensive devotion to the Lord and the concerns of spiritual life. This devotion is expressed by abstaining for a short while from such normal and good things as food and drink. It allows you to enjoy a time of uninterrupted communion with our Father.

We have confidence to enter the Most Holy Place by the blood of Jesus.
(Hebrews 10:19, NIV)

The privilege to enter the presence of God, whether fasting or not, is one of the most delightful parts of that better thing, which is ours in Christ. Prayer and fasting should not be a burden or duty. Rather, it should be a celebration of God's goodness and mercy to His children.

Jesus said to His disciples, "This kind can come out by nothing but fasting and prayer" (Mark 9:29). You may ask what kind Jesus was referring to. Who was Jesus referring to? The fact is the kind of demon the disciples were facing could only come out of the possessed body through fasting and prayer.

What Is Fasting?

Fasting is when people choose to abstain from food to deepen their spiritual growth due to an overwhelming spiritual hunger. The Greek word *nesteuo* and Hebrew word *tsum* mean to abstain from food. If a person is said to be in fasting, he/she sacrifices the desires of the flesh (food) for the things of the spirit (meditation, fasting, and prayer). Fasting breaks the chains of bondage and frees us from the things which bind us to the world of materialism and our surroundings.

Fasting enables people to refocus their attention on the things of God and His commandments. It causes us to face and overcome the enemy's plan. Jesus Himself said:

> *It is written: Man shall not live on bread alone, but on every word, that comes from the mouth of God.* (Matthew 4:4, NIV)

While men may live on substances (such as bread) as food for the physical body, God supports both the physical and spiritual life by other means. God, who is the Word, feeds us with His Word; therefore, in a period of fasting, we too must study and meditate on the Word of God, which comes from God Himself.

Jesus saw the importance and the necessity of fasting. Jesus fasted before He was tempted by Satan (Matthew 4:1-11). He fasted 40 days and nights (Matthew 4:2) before commencing His public ministry. Personal attacks came after His fasting (Matthew 4:3, 6, 9). However, despite the personal attacks and Jesus' physical weakness, He was spiritually strong and well-prepared for the temptation.

Therefore, fasting brings spiritual strength to combat the temptations that will arise.

Fasting must be sincere. The book of Isaiah highlights how Isaiah rebuked the nation of Israel for their insincere fast.

Why have we fasted they say, and you have not seen it? Why have we humbled ourselves, and you have not noticed. Yet on the day of your fasting, you do as you please and exploit all your workers. Your fasting ends in quarrelling and strife, and in striking each other with wicked fists. You cannot fast as you do today and expect your voice to be heard on high. Is this the kind of fast I have chosen, only a day for people to humble themselves? Is it only for bowing one's head like a reed and for lying in sackcloth and ashes? Is that what you call a fast, a day acceptable to the Lord? Is not this the kind of fasting I have chosen: to loose the chains of injustice and untie the cords of the yoke, to set the oppressed free and break every yoke? (Isaiah 58:3-6, NIV)

Why Should Fasting and Prayer Be Combined?

For fasting to be effective it must be accompanied by prayer. Therefore, fasting should not be simply a non-eating exercise. According to research, fasting has many health benefits: weight loss, reduced cholesterol, and lower blood pressure. Fasting must be combined with prayer; otherwise, it will become more of a health-conscious activity to reduce weight loss than a spiritual encounter. Fasting and prayer are important Christian spiritual disciplines that are applicable to every Christian.

For example, Daniel prayed to the Lord while fasting in sackcloth and ashes because of the desolation of Jerusalem.

So, I turned to the Lord God and pleaded with him in prayer and petition, in fasting, and in sackcloth and ashes. (Daniel 9:3, NIV)

Daniel's prayer and fasting were a heavy plea to God to have mercy upon the people because of their sins and turning away from Him.

We have sinned and done wrong. We have been wicked and have rebelled, we have turned away from your commands and laws.

(Daniel 9:5, NIV)

So, we need to fast, pray, and ask God to have mercy on us.

Fasting and prayer are also Christian spiritual disciplines to seek God's guidance. Doing so was important for the appointing of leaders in the New Testament. When Paul and Barnabas required elders for each church in Antioch in Syria, they combined fasting and prayer. Then they committed the elders to the Lord in whom they had put their confidence.

Paul and Barnabas appointed elders for them in each church and, with prayer and fasting, committed them to the Lord, in whom they had put their trust. (Acts 14:23, NIV)

How to Fast as a Christian

Fasting is a sacred time when Christians abstain from *food* or *other pleasures* and take the time to focus on God. When you fast, do so with the *right motives*. You must do this to *humble yourself* before Him. It is a way to glorify our Lord, not ourselves. Keep these aspects in mind while you fast. Don't confuse this with any other reasons for fasting such as weight loss; center it on Jesus.

Before You Fast

Pray, confess your sins, and ask the Holy Spirit to lead you. Let Jesus know you want to know Him personally. Acknowledge that He lived without sin and died in our place on the cross for our sins. He rose 3 days later freeing us from condemnation and giving us His free gift of eternal life. Humble yourself and ask forgiveness from everyone you have hurt; ask forgiveness from God. Forgive those who have hurt you. You do not want to enter a fast, *holding grudges*, carrying *envy, pride, anger,* or *hurt.* The enemy will try to use those things to distract you from your fast.

Meditate on the scriptures and on the holy traits of our Lord. These may include the ability to *forgive*, His strength or wisdom, His peace, the capacity to love unconditionally, etc. Praise Him for these attributes! Surrender your life and thank Him for all He has done for you!

Determine the length of your fasting experience: one meal, one day, 3 days, or more. You may wish to try a shorter fast and start slowly if you have not previously fasted. You can also pray and ask the Holy Spirit to reveal to you how long you should fast.

Note the type of fast you are being called to. You may feel the Holy Spirit is calling you to a specific type of fast. It may be restricting your food intake, which may include a juice diet, vegetable, fruit, or water. Always use precautions. Drink an adequate amount of water to prevent dehydration. Consult your physician prior to fasting.

In an absolute fast, one abstains from solid and liquid foods (fruit juices are foods). Drink enough water to support life; it is not food. However, water is essential for life as much as breathing is; therefore, you should drink adequate amounts of water during your fast. Failure to do so for long periods may negatively affect your mental state, send you into a coma, or you may die after a mere 4 or 5 days of dehydration.

During the Fast

- Hold Morning Worship – While fasting, you can hold morning worship. Worship God and praise Him for His attributes. Read His Word and meditate. Ask God for wisdom so you can input His Word into your life and gain a fuller understanding of it. Pray for God's will to be done and for the guidance of the Holy Spirit. Ask God to lead you in spreading His glory into the world we live in.

- Go for a Prayer Walk – Walk outside hand-in-hand with nature while noticing God's wondrous creation. Thank Him for everything He has made as you walk. Ask Him to give you a spirit of thanksgiving and appreciation.

- Pray for Others – Pray for church leaders to preach God's Word as He intended, so your friends and family members will grow closer to Him or accept Him into their lives. Pray for government leaders to come to God and seek His guidance and direction in governing the affairs of the people.

After the Fast

- Continue to pray without ceasing
- Avoid gorging yourself after fasting
- The first day, gradually add in a raw salad after breaking your fast
- The second day, add a baked potato, avoiding any fat or salt on it
- The third day, add steamed vegetables.
- Afterward, progressively add more healthy food into your diet

Specific Prayer Points While Fasting

(Taken from *A Powerful Prayer Life* by Gregory Frizzell)

- Ask God to bring deep conviction of sin, spiritual brokenness, a holy fear of God, and genuine repentance among His people. There will be no revival without these elements and only God can produce them in His people. After all, we cannot program or work up genuine brokenness and repentance (2 Corinthians 7:10)

- Pray for deep cleansing, genuine repentance, and spiritual power to engulf pastors and Christian leaders. Revival and spiritual awakening are extremely unlikely without a mighty move of God in pastors and Christian leaders. Renewed pastors are absolutely crucial to a move of God in our day! (Ephesians 6:14-20)

- Pray for God to bestow spiritual hunger in His people and draw them to fervent intercession. God has to grant people the genuine faith and the fervent desire for prayer. We cannot produce a genuine prayer movement with all our promotion and programming (Philippians 2:13)

- Pray that God will bring unity into our churches and a deep harmony between them. Many churches need healing among members and to stop competing jealously with each other (John 13:35)

- Pray for God to fill His people with a passion to see others saved. Only God can give a genuine burden for souls. Until God's people intensely pray for the lost and do aggressive soul-winning, revival will tarry. Be sure you are constantly praying for many lost people by name (Romans 9:1-3)

- Pray for God to give His people a passion for missions and starting churches. Great revivals produce an explosion of mission projects, new ministries, and new church starts. Only God can grant a genuine passion for missions (Matthew 28:19)

- Pray that God will call thousands into ministry, missions, and Christian service. Many churches are dying because of a lack of soul winners, teachers, and church workers. Furthermore, we can only start as many churches as the church planters we have to start them (Matthew 9:37)

- Pray that God will pour out His Spirit like a mighty purifying flood. Ask God to purify our motives as we pray for revival. After all, it is possible to pray for revival for selfish or ambitious reasons

- Our motives must be solely for (a) the glory of God, and (b) the increase of the kingdom of God. We must not pray for revival just to solve our own problems or make our church successful in the eyes of men (James 4:2)

- Pray for a mighty move of conviction and salvation upon communities of cultural influence. Some key examples are Hollywood actors and producers, government officials, educators, teachers, college professors, news and media people, talk shows hosts, comedians, homosexual activist groups, and the music industry (1 Timothy 2:1-2)

- Specifically pray for God to pour out His Spirit (Mark 11:22-24; John 14:13-14)

The Fast Life

Fast from judging others; feast on Christ dwelling in them

Fast from fear of illness; feast on the healing power of God

Fast from words that pollute; feast on speech that purifies

Fast from discontent; feast on gratitude

Fast from anger; feast on patience

Fast from pessimism; feast on hope

Fast from negatives; feast on encouragement

Fast from bitterness; feast on forgiveness

Fast from self-concern; feast on compassion

Fast from suspicion; feast on truth

Fast from gossip; feast on purposeful silence

Fast from problems that overwhelm; feast on prayer that sustains

Fast from anxiety; feast on faith

[Author Unknown]

Conclusion

Let us become a people of prayer who seek the face of God and call upon Him. Let us cultivate a lifestyle of Spirit-empowered prayer!

For the weapons of our warfare are not carnal but mighty through God to the pulling down strongholds, casting down imaginations and every high thing that exalts itself against the knowledge of God and bringing into captivity every thought to the obedience of Christ, and having a readiness to revenge all disobedience when your obedience is fulfilled. (2 Corinthians 10:4-6)

Appendix A

WHAT DOES PRAYER MEAN TO ME?

A Child's Perspective – (Ages 3-5)

Prayer is talking to God. — Christmas

Prayer is when you talk to Jesus. — Dalina

Prayer is talking to God. — Jaden

Prayer is telling God to help us. — Rhema

Prayer is talking to and blessing God. — Skylar

A Youth's Perspective – (Ages 6-17)

Prayer is talking to God and bringing all your problems to Him, listening and making a bond. — Devon Banks

Prayer is talking to God and sharing all your information with Him.
— Xavier Crowder

Prayer means I can talk to God by myself. — Faith

Prayer is talking to the Lord about what has been going on in my life and giving glory to the Lord because He forgives sin. — Kani

Prayer is a way of talking to Jesus. — Jessii

Prayer is listening to God's Word when you pray every day and do it.
— George Rodriquez

Prayer is to talk to God and understand the Word of God. — TB

Prayer is a conversation you have with Jesus. It is also a way to boost your mood because you cast all your cares upon Him. — Ayanna Thompson

A Young Adult's Perspective — (Ages 18-34)

Prayer is communication between someone and God. — Aja

Prayer is talking and listening to God. — Danielle Bush

Prayer is the believer's way to communicate with God. Prayer shows both love and confidence in God that He will hear our prayers and give an answer in His time. — Justin Funchess

Prayer is a conversation with God. It should include humbly acknowledging God's power, asking for forgiveness, praying for the needs of others, and asking for your needs. — Cortez Hadley

Prayer is a conversation with God where you ask for forgiveness, guidance, and protection. — Steven McDonald, Jr.

Prayer is having a talk with the Lord, and it is a conversation with God.
— Anthony Morris

An Adult's Perspective — (Ages 35-59)

Prayer is talking to God with the Spirit He gave me to share what is on my heart. — Ontario Bowen

Prayer is asking for His help in my daily walk. Just letting Him know I am thankful that He is part of my life. — La Shoney Young

Prayer is communicating with God, such as listening and talking.
— Harlum Drake

Prayer to me is communicating with God orally, worshipping, praising, and confessing my sin. — Felicia Louden

Prayer to me is communicating with the Father, no matter what is going on around me. — Theresa Boyce

Prayer is the most important thing that starts my day. It becomes so necessary that I talk to God and allow Him to give me directions. Sometimes it is a struggle, but it is comforting to lift up the name of Jesus in my prayer time. — Tannesha Carpenter

Prayer means a lot to me. I can go to God and make my requests known. He gives me what He wants for me. I like the fact that I can call on God at any time, even in my weakest hour. He knows what I need even before I ask. He is merciful, kind, and loving. I am so thankful for His grace and mercy. — Valerie Emmons

Prayer is fellowship with God. I pray because God created us to communicate with Him and seek His will. Prayer is important to me because it is God's will that all would come to Him. I plan to petition more for the present conditions and passionate pleas for God's help. — Christopher C. Robinson Sr., Interim Pastor

Prayer is having a conversation with God where I can pray and listen, praise and worship. — Andrea Ward

Prayer is communicating with the Lord; it is a time of fellowship, praise, and worship with God. — Avire Lawson

A Senior Adult's Perspective – (Ages 60 and up)

Prayer is being able to go to Him at any time to talk to Him about everything. I can ask Him for guidance and understanding of whatever I am going through. — Archie Banks

Prayer is talking to God about everything, thanking and obeying Him.
— Juliette Brown

Prayer is precious. When I think about prayer, I think about Jesus when He said men should always pray and not faint. We should pray with expectation, knowing that God hears and answers prayer.

— Herman Duffin, Midday Pastor

Prayer to me is a way of talking to the Most High God. Giving to Him my concerns and worries through our Lord Jesus Christ, knowing that He will keep me strong. — Claudette Hendricks

Prayer is my personal and special time with the God of my salvation. My time to say thank You for saving me and choosing me to be an intercessor, to pray for others who are in need. — Willie Johnson

Prayer is talking to God, telling Him all about my troubles. Thanking Him for who He is, asking Him for His blessings and mercy upon everyone.

—DeloresMatt

Prayer is the most important thing in a Christian's life. — Cal Means

Prayer is talking with and listening to the Lord as He leads and guides me to impart or share my praise of Him and my requests to Him. So as to live a life worthy of my calling as a Christian. — Melvin Mullins

Prayer is thanking God for His goodness. — Deacon Carl Pettigrew

Prayer to me means talking to God on a daily basis, including Him in everything that is going on in my life. It is a time for He and I to spend quiet time together. — Kathy Rates

Prayer is a privilege and honor to communicate with my heavenly Father, thanking, praising, worshipping, and interceding for others, as well as offering up my petitions for my needs and wants. — Catherine Scott

Prayer is the means by which we give glory to God, and the way we communicate with Him. — J. Sorrell

Prayer to me has this exciting mixture of familiarity and awe. I get to talk with and hear from God who loves me and is so close to me, yet so holy and far removed from me. Prayer keeps me humble and focused on heaven. A major change I made was to put God first. Going forward, I want to increase my prayer time by being consistent. I want to put Him first (early in the morning) and last (late at night).

— Robert C. Walker, Missions Pastor

Prayer is a way of communicating with God about concerns we have about others. — Deacon Henry Wilson

Prayer is spending time with God. It is talking to God. Not only do we talk to Him, but we must also find time to listen to what the Holy Spirit is saying to us. — Anonymous

PRAYERS FOR EVERYDAY LIVING

Pray for the Children

God has a plan for children. God wants to use *you* to defeat the enemy. But you need to draw near to God where you distinguish between the *real* and the *counterfeit*. Also, know that the absence of social and moral values opens the door for the entrance of demons into your life.

Prayer for Children

Heavenly Father, we exalt You and praise Your holy name. You are worthy to be praised. No one can measure Your greatness. Father, it is Your will that our children prosper and have good success. We pray that they will trust and obey You. Let them put You first in all that they do. We cry out for the children all around the world. Help them to obey the voice of the Lord and walk uprightly before You.

Father, thank You for raising mentors to help the children with their homework, talk, listen, and be involved in their lives. Fill their hearts with wisdom, knowledge, and understanding. Help them to choose godly friends and bless their relationships with their parents and loved ones. Send laborers in the vineyard to minister to the parents and the children. Turn their hearts toward You. Give the parents wisdom and patience as they diligently teach their children Your Word. Teach the parents Your principles and precepts for training their children in the way they should go.

Remind the children to listen to sound advice and follow godly instructions.

Teach them not to defile themselves with the ways of the world through for-nication, lying, stealing, alcohol and drug abuse, and other worldly things. Help them to walk in the fruit of the Spirit. Protect them while they are at school from bullies and the evil one. Cover them with the blood of Jesus. Thank You, Lord, for hearing our prayers. In Jesus' name, I pray. Amen.

Scripture: Ephesians 6:1; Proverbs 22:6

Pray for Those Who Are Grieving

Grief is a natural response to loss. It is the emotional suffering one feels when something or someone we love is taken away. Grief is also a reaction to any loss. The grief associated with death is familiar to most people, but individuals grieve for a variety of losses throughout their lives: unemployment, ill health, or the end of a relationship.

Loss can be categorized as either physical or abstract. Physical loss is related to something the individual can touch or measure such as losing a spouse through death. Other types of losses are abstract and relate to aspects of a person's social interactions. Whatever the situation, everyone grieves differently. As a believer, you can turn to God's Word to find strength and comfort while you are grieving.

Prayer for Grieving Families

Father, I pray for [name one or more] and other family and friends who are grieving. They are hurting for many reasons, and I ask You to help them through this season of loss. You know the pain and sorrow they are going through. Father, hear our prayer for those who mourn the death of their beloved. Comfort them as they go through the grief process. You promised to never leave or forsake them.

You are the God who comforts them as they go through their struggles. Let them know You are able to see them through. Strengthen them so they can help others who face the same struggles. When they are hurting, help them find their joy in You. Your joy will be their strength. Help them to put their trust in You.

Lord, God, pour Your Holy Spirit into their lives. Fill them with Your love and compassion, so they may see their brothers and sisters as You see them and be equipped to carry out their appointed duties.

Lord, God, we pray for all of Your people. Fill them with Your joy, peace, and hope by the power of the Holy Spirit. Help them experience the love, joy, and peace that are the result of Your life in them, no matter what they are going through. May they sense Your presence in this hour of need. In Jesus' name, I pray. Amen.

> *Scripture: 1 Samuel 20:14a; 2 Corinthians 1:3–4; Galatians 5:22: Nehemiah 8:10 b: Psalm 33:22: Romans 15:13*

Pray for Healing

There are different types of healing mentioned in the Bible: physical healing, emotional healing, and spiritual healing. The Bible touches on several aspects of health and healing. There is no formula on how to pray for healing, but there are many Scripture verses we can use to pray for it. We just need to learn what the Bible has to say about healing and pray accordingly.

The following prayer is for *physical healing* of sicknesses and diseases. Prior to praying the prayer, try to read and meditate on these Scripture verses below. They will help to build your faith.

Repent of all sins and ask God to forgive you. Read and meditate on the Scripture verses below:

Is anyone among you in trouble? Let them pray. Is anyone happy? Let them sing songs of praise. Is anyone among you sick? Let them call the elders of the church to pray over them and anoint them with oil in the name of the Lord. And the prayer offered in faith will make the sick person well; the Lord will raise them up. If they have sinned, they will be forgiven. (James 5:13-15, KJV)

Those who hope in the Lord will renew their strength. They will soar on wings like eagles; they will run and not grow weary they will walk and not be faint. (Isaiah 40:31, KJV)

I will restore you to health and heal your wounds, declares the LORD, because you are called an outcast, Zion for whom no one cares. (Jeremiah 30:17, KJV)

Then they cried to the Lord in their trouble, and he saved them from their distress. He sent out his word and healed them; he rescued them from the grave. (Psalm 107:6, KJV)

Praise the Lord, my soul; all my inmost being, praise his holy name. Praise the LORD, my soul, and forget not all His benefits, who forgives all your sins and heals all your diseases, who redeems your life from the pit and crowns you with love and compassion, who satisfies your desires with good things so that your youth is renewed like the eagle's. (Psalm 103:1-5, KJV)

Praise and thank God for your healing. Repeat the process each day.

General Prayer

Father God, we know You have all power in Your hands. Even as we have voiced our particular concern for these people, we are aware each one of them has a different need. We know some of these needs but not others. Lord, You know everything. You are omniscient—all-knowing. May the healing and restoring power of Your Holy Spirit permeate each one of them, fulfilling Your desire that they may experience abundant life.

It is our privilege to give You thanks and praise, acknowledging You give life, health, and wholeness. Thank You for ministering to us in this experience. Make us ever mindful of Your mercies so as we praise You, we may continue to be faithful servants of Jesus Christ. In Jesus' name, we pray. Amen.

Prayer for Inner Healing

Heavenly Father, I come before You now in great need of Your mercy. You are the doctor and physician of my soul. I humbly beseech You to send forth Your healing power into every area of my inner-being. I surrender all to You, Lord. Remove anger, bitterness, unforgiveness, and a hurtful past that is causing harm to my physical health.

I ask for Your grace to forgive every person in my past who has ever hurt me. I forgive my father and mother. Set me free from all forms of mental, emotional, and psychological ailments. I forgive my brothers and sisters for their sibling rivalry, selfishness, and divisiveness that have caused strife within our family. I forgive my friends, coworkers, and neighbors for all their harmful actions and the unkind words they have spoken against me.

I forgive my spouse, children, and all my extended family members. I ask for Your loving grace to heal all the circumstances where I failed to receive the love, affection, support, and respect I needed. I forgive all those who have violated my sexual purity. Set me free and wash me clean by the blood of the Lamb. I forgive myself for my past mistakes and failures. Liberate me from all destructive consequences, guilt, shame, and self-condemnation.

I forgive all those in positions of authority, especially those [say only what applies to you] doctors, nurses, healthcare providers, insurance adjustors, paramedics, police officers, government officials, former employers, and members of the clergy who have treated me unjustly. I forgive my greatest enemies and those I vowed I would never forgive.

Through the power of Your Holy Spirit, I ask You, Lord Jesus, to fill me with Your love, peace, patience, kindness, generosity, and self-control. May Your healing hand rest upon me now as I bless all those who have hurt me. I desire to be kind and compassionate to everyone, forgiving them just as You have forgiven me. I ask for the healing power of Your love to flow through every cell of my body and into the lives of those whom I have forgiven. In Jesus' name, I pray. Amen.

Prayer for Mental Healing

Heavenly Father, You are the great I AM. You are worthy to be praised.

You are to be feared above all gods. The earth is Yours and everything in it; the world and all its people belong to You. You are the King of Glory, the Lord strong and mighty. We are grateful that when we, Your people, call to You for help. You hear and understand. Allow us to seek Your will for our lives. Bring rest to our souls. We trust in Your Word and believe it will operate in the hearts and souls of those with mental illnesses.

We confess that when they walk in the midst of trouble, You will revive them, stretch forth Your hand, and save them. You have left Your gift of peace of mind with them, and we pray their hearts will not be afraid. We confess that although they may be pressed on every side by trouble, they will not be crushed and broken. They may feel perplexed, but they will not give up and quit. They may be knocked down, but You will never abandon them. They will get up and keep going. Father, we confess that they will lie down without fear and enjoy pleasant dreams. They will not be afraid of the threat of disaster or destruction, for You are their security.

Holy Spirit, we ask You to replace sadness with joy, defeat with victory, and fatigue with praise. Help those who feel depressed or sad not to focus on their circumstances but on Your blessings in their lives. Remind them to praise You at all times. We ask You to bring all things to their memory that concern You and Your plans for their lives. Give them power as they meditate on Your Word. Help them to keep Your commandments and embrace them in their hearts. Father, help them not to conform to this world but to be transformed by the renewing of their minds through Your Word.

Holy Spirit, strengthen and renew their innermost beings. Let the fiery darts of the enemy not permeate their beings. May they always hear Your voice and obey Your will. Father, please help them to overcome their fears. Please strengthen their family members and caretakers. Help them to always walk in Your peace and love with their loved ones. Rescue them out of their troubles.

Thank You for giving us Your peace and joy. Thank You for providing a life of hope, abundance, and destiny. Thank You for being our strength in times of trouble. In Jesus' name, I pray. Amen.

Scripture: Psalm 18:1-31, 42

Prayer for Physical Healing

Heavenly Father, You said You will give rest to all who are weary and heavy burdened. Your yoke is easy and Your burdens are light. Help me to trust You with all of my heart and lean not on my own understanding. As You were with Moses, so are You with me. No evil will befall me. No plague will come near my dwelling. For You have given Your angels charge over me. They keep me in all my ways (Psalm 91:10-11).

In my pathway are life, healing, and health. Therefore, I refuse to allow sickness to dominate my body. The blood of Jesus flows within me, bringing healing to every fiber of my being. I am redeemed from the curse because Christ became a curse for me. As your Word says cursed is anyone who hangs on a tree. The blood of Jesus covers and protects me. It flows to every cell of my body, restoring life and health.

My body is the temple of the Holy Ghost. I pray for a release of the right chemicals and hormones so my body is in perfect balance. My pancreas secretes the proper amount of insulin for life and health. I pray that every [name your illness example] cancer, and abnormal cell is uprooted from my body now and replaced by cells perfected by the Spirit of God.

I attend to Your Word. I incline my ears to Your sayings. I will not let them depart from my eyes. I will keep them in the midst of my heart, for they are life and healing to my flesh. I decree Your Word over my body right now. I shall not die but live and declare the works of the Lord. In Jesus' name, I pray. Amen.

Prayer for Healing (Coronavirus)

Heavenly Father, we thank You for the power of prayer. You are the Great Physician, Jehovah Rapha (God who heals). We lift up all the people who have been affected by the coronavirus. Comfort those who are in quarantine. Remove the virus from those who are infected, in Jesus' name. Touch them and their families with Your healing hands of mercy. Holy Spirit, thank You for being a consuming fire. Burn out everything that is not like You.

Restore every cell, the sense of smell and taste, as well as every infected part of their beings. We come against all respiratory illnesses, shortness of breath, asthma, emphysema, bronchitis, inflammation of the lungs, and all infections. We pray there will be no lasting effects from this virus. Heal them from the inside out.

We thank You, Lord, for the wisdom and knowledge You have given the scientists, disease experts, and epidemiologists who have worked hard to come up with a vaccine. Thank You for the medical staff of doctors, nurses, healthcare workers, and caregivers. Renew their strength. In Jesus' name, we pray. Amen.

Prayer for the Incarcerated

Father, we thank You for those who are incarcerated. Thank You for the life lessons they are learning through the various ministries.

Thank You for giving them another chance to start over again. Give them repentant hearts. Create in them clean hearts and renew the right spirit within them. Allow a change to take place in their spirits that they may be transformed by the renewing of their minds.

Thank You, Lord, for Your grace and mercy that covers, protects, prepares, and equips them to return to society. Father, we pray that after they are paroled, church members will not treat them like outcasts, but they will receive them into the house of God. Prepare them to be ready to start a new life in Christ. Let them make a difference in the world and walk in the newness of life. In Jesus' name, we pray. Amen.

Prayer for Marriages

Heavenly Father, we lift our marriages up to You. We understand that our union is a picture of our relationship with You. Let our thoughts agree with Your will so we may have good success in our marriage relationship. Help us to be kind and tenderhearted, forgiving, and loving to one another. Help us to speak the truth in love and listen to each other.

Strengthen us where we are weak and build us up where we are torn down. Allow us to believe You for the impossible. Help us to pray together, trust in You, and walk in obedience to Your Word, so we may have peace and joy. Let us love, honor, and respect each other.

Forgive us for our self-centeredness, anger, lust, and foolishness. Let us be swift to hear and slow to speak, so we will not blame or accuse one another. Let us see You as our source and provision. Restore the areas where our hearts are broken. Deliver us from rejection and sorrow. Today, we choose to receive Your healing, love, forgiveness, joy, faithfulness, and self-control into our lives.

We choose not to deprive each other of sexual love and remain faithful to our own mates. Remove the blinders from our eyes, so we can see the truth and walk courageously in it. We resist the enemy who will try to destroy our marriages.

We bind every hindering spirit that will come against this marriage, in the name of Jesus. We invite the Holy Spirit into our lives where we can worship You and grow in the knowledge of Your will. In Jesus' name, we pray. Amen.

Prayer for a Missing Person

Heavenly Father, 'I will lift up mine eyes unto the hills, from whence cometh my help. My help cometh from the Lord, which made heaven and earth' (Psalm 121:1-2).

Lord, we cry out to You on behalf of those who are missing as we patiently await their safe return or to hear news of their whereabouts. You said, 'Be careful for nothing; but in everything by prayer and supplication with thanksgiving let your requests be made known unto God' (Philippians 4:6).

You promised to never leave us or forsake us. Therefore, we continue to trust You at Your Word and hope in the miracle working power of the Holy Spirit. We trust You, Lord Jesus, for the safe return of [name the person].

You are the great I AM. You are omnipresent (everywhere at the same time), and You know where our loved ones are right now.

We surrender all of our fearful thoughts to You. For we know 'God hath not given us the spirit of fear but of power, and of love, and of a sound mind' (2 Timothy 1:7).

We call upon Your perfect wisdom to guide everything to ensure our loved ones' complete safety and protection. We know Your love ensures our safety and well-being; there is nothing to fear. Please take our fears and turn them into joy for the joy of the Lord is our strength. Thank You, in advance, for their safe and immediate return. In Jesus' name, we pray. Amen.

Prayer for the Nation

Heavenly Father, You alone are the Lord of the earth and King of the universe. You alone can revive and restore the United States of America and bring it back under your sovereign rule. Give our president, his advisors, and the whole of his administration the wisdom and grace to turn from the ungodly path they are following. May they set this nation back on the path of trusting in God. Motivate all our congressional leaders to strive for integrity and wisdom in all the choices and decisions they make. May those entrusted as judges and lawmakers act in righteousness, impartiality, and integrity as they work for the benefit of all people and to the honor of Your holy name.

Father, Your Word says, 'Blessed is the nation whose God is the Lord' (Psalm 33:12). Thus, we place our nation at Your feet and pray we will once again serve You. May Your will be done in the once greatest nation of the world— the United States of America. In Jesus' name, we pray. Amen.

Prayer for Protection

Father, I thank You for Your hand of protection over my family, friends, and me. You watch over Your Word to perform it. I thank You that my family, friends, and I dwell in the secret place of the Most High and that we remain stable and fixed under the shadow of the Almighty. I cover my family, friends, and me with the precious blood of Jesus.

Father, You are our refuge and fortress. No evil shall befall us. No accident shall overtake us. No plague or calamity shall come near our home. Encamp Your angels all around us. Shelter us from the storm and keep us from all destruction. Father, give us the peace of God, which surpasses all understanding. Help us to stand firm and not compromise Your Word. Keep us forever close to Your heart. In Jesus' name, I pray. Amen.

Scripture: Philippians 4:7; Psalm 91

Salvation Scriptures

For all have sinned and come short of the glory of God. (Romans 3:23, KJV)

For the wages of sin is death; but the gift of God is eternal life through Jesus Christ our Lord. (Romans 6:23, KJV)

For God so loved the world that he gave his only begotten son that whoever believes in him shall not perish but have eternal life. (John 3:16, KJV)

Jesus said, I am the way, the truth, and the life: no man comes to the Father, but by me. (John 14:6, KJV)

Steps to Salvation

That if thou shalt confess with thy mouth the Lord Jesus, and shalt believe in thine heart that God hath raised him from the dead, thou shalt be saved. For with the heart man believeth unto righteousness; and with the mouth confession is made unto salvation. (Romans 10:9-10, KJV)

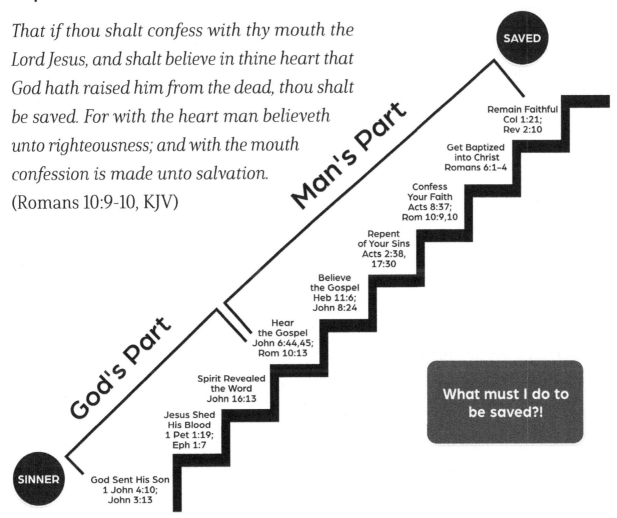

The Only Way to Heaven Is Through Jesus Christ

- Hear the Word of God

  So then faith cometh by hearing and hearing the word of God.
  (Romans 10:17, KJV)

- Believe that Jesus is the Son of God

  For God so loved the world, that he gave his only begotten Son, that whosoever believeth in him should not perish, but have everlasting life. (John 3:16, KJV)

- Repent of your sins

  Repent ye therefore, and be converted, that your sins may be blotted out, when the times of refreshing shall come from the presence of the Lord. (Acts 3:19, KJV)

- Confess the name of Christ

  That if thou shalt confess with thy mouth the Lord Jesus, and shalt believe in thine heart that God hath raised him from the dead, thou shalt be saved. (Romans 10:9, KJV)

- Be baptized in water

  What shall we say then? Shall we continue in sin, that grace may abound? God forbid. How shall we, that are dead to sin, live any longer therein? Know ye not, that so many of us as were baptized into Jesus Christ were baptized into his death? Therefore, we are buried with him by baptism into death: that like as Christ was raised up from the dead by the glory of the Father, even so we also should walk in newness of life. (Romans 6:1-4, KJV)

- Live faithfully unto death

But grow in grace and in the knowledge of our Lord and Savior Jesus Christ. To him be glory both now and forever. Amen. (2 Peter 3:18, KJV)

But speaking the truth in love, may grow up into him in all things, which is the head, even Christ. (Ephesians 4:15, KJV)

Prayer for Salvation

If you want to be assured of eternal salvation today, just pray this simple prayer with sincerity, humility, and from the bottom of your soul. Read it if you need to but *mean it*!

Dear Jesus, I believe in You. I believe You are the only begotten Son of God. I believe You shed Your blood and died for my sins; You were buried and rose again as it is written in the Scriptures. I am sorry for the things I have done that hurt You. Forgive me for all my sins, Lord Jesus.

Come into my heart today. Take charge of my life and fill me with Your Holy Spirit. I renounce all my sinful practices of the past. Cleanse my heart with Your precious blood. I believe that You are the way the truth and the life. You are the only way to salvation. I surrender my will and my life to You. Fill me with Your Holy Spirit. In Jesus Christ's name, I pray. Amen.

Prayer for Singles

Father God, I come before Your holy throne lifting up the singles. You said, 'If any of you lack wisdom let him ask of God, that giveth to all men liberally, and upbraideth not; and it shall be given him' (James 1:5, KJV).

Lord, I confess I have sinned and fallen short of Your glory, but I thank You for being a forgiving God who looks beyond my faults and sees my need. I repent of all my sins and ask You to forgive me. Create in me a clean heart and renew the right spirit within me (Psalm 51:10).

I realize that I do not deserve Your mercy or grace. I am not worthy to gather the crumbs from under Your table. I thank You that I have been redeemed by the blood of the Lamb. I am able to approach Your throne for grace and find strength. I need Your strength to keep me from falling, to walk in Your ways, and live godly in Christ Jesus. I pray You will lead and guide me by Your Holy Spirit, so I may walk in the newness of life.

Grant me a love for the Lord that consumes all my heart, soul, and mind. Help me to love others as I love myself (Matthew 22:37-39). Enable me to keep my heart with all diligence, for out of it flows the issues of life (Proverbs 4:23). Show me the areas I need to correct [confess and forsake any sin He reveals].

I ask You, dear Lord, to look down on all men and women who have an inner yearning and desire to be married but are single. Look with compassion on the desires of their hearts and bring people to them with whom they can share their lives and future, in Jesus' name.

Father, guard their hearts and minds during the time of waiting. Give them the peace of God that surpasses all understanding. Let their lives be examples of You. In Jesus' name, I pray. Amen.

Scripture: 2 Timothy 2:15; Matthew 6:33; Psalm 51:10

Prayer for Widows, Widowers, Orphans, and the Homeless

Heavenly Father, in the name of Jesus, we pray for the widows, widowers, orphans, and the homeless. We pray that You will be the spouse, sibling, friend, mother, and father of them all. Cover them with Your love. When they feel all hope is gone, renew them with joy and peace. May the bond of love You have for Your people be the foundation of their hope because love never fails. Allow them to forever hold on to the precious memories of their loved ones.

May Your Holy Spirit give them inner strength, courage, and joy. Raise their expectation. Help them to live with passion and purpose letting the world know that to live is Christ and to die is gain. Help them to believe You for the impossible. Let them know You will complete the work You are doing in their lives. Give them spiritual insight and wisdom to discern what is best for them in the midst of their sadness.

Keep them pure and blameless. Fill them with the fruit of righteousness. In the name of Jesus. Encamp Your angels all around them to protect them. Bless their families and friends in a mighty way, in the name of Jesus. Father, forgive the ones who reject them and cause them pain. Let the words of their mouths and the meditation of their hearts be acceptable in Your sight. You are their strength and Redeemer. In Jesus' name, we pray. Amen.

Scripture: 1 Corinthians 13:8; Philippians 1:21; Psalm 19:14, 91

Prayer for Young People

Father, we thank You for forgiving us our sins and cleansing us from all unrighteousness. We come, not in our own righteousness but in the righteousness of Jesus Christ. We lift up the youth and young adults. Keep, protect, shield, strengthen, comfort, teach, correct, and love them. Give them the strength to say "No" to drugs, sex, and alcohol, following the wrong crowd, and hanging out when they should be in class.

Father, our youth are faced with so much peer pressure today. So we come interceding on their behalf asking You to put a hedge of protection around them.

Some of our youth live in troubled homes. We ask You for divine intervention in their lives. Open doors and provide their needs. Some are hurting and heartbroken, but we thank You, Lord, for being a forgiving God.

Lord, build their confidence and encourage their hearts. Bring healing, deliverance, forgiveness, reconciliation, and restoration. Thank You for restoring the homes today, giving wisdom to the parents, and turning the hearts of fathers and mothers to You that they may show more love to their children.

Father, You said all have sinned and come short of the glory of God. We thank You for being a forgiving God. Forgive our youth for being rebellious and disrespectful to their parents, teachers, elders, and those in authority. Forgive them for not obeying the instruction of their parents. Forgive them for using profanity, viewing pornographic movies and books, not studying, fornicating, gossiping, ridiculing others, and not representing the kingdom of God in their daily living.

Forgive the parents for not raising their youth according to Your ways. Forgive parents for provoking their youth to anger by falsely accusing them, cursing them, or using profanity. Forgive parents and youth for not representing the kingdom of God in their homes. Lord, remind parents and youth to forgive one another and others.

Lord, Your Word is forever settled in heaven. There is no God like You. Your Word is perfect. You are our strong tower, fortress, and place of refuge. You have done marvelous things. We give You praise. To the only wise God, be the glory, majesty, dominion, and power both now and forever. In Jesus' name, I pray. Amen.

Scripture: Colossians 1:9; Daniel 1:17-20; Deuteronomy 6:6-9; Ephesians 3:18, 6:4; Galatians 5:22; Jude 1:24-25; Malachi 4:6; Matthew 6:13, 33; Proverbs 3:4, 22:6; Psalm 119:89, 145:1, 3-4, 9-10, 150:2; Romans 10:9.

Christian Testimonials of Answered Prayer

YOLANDA'S TESTIMONY

I had a wonderful childhood. I was born in Chicago, Illinois. My relationship with my parents was great.

My Life Before Christ

Question: How did your non-spiritual state affect your feelings, thoughts, attitudes, and relationships?

Answer: Before my life with Christ, I found myself searching for purpose and meaning in people and also in myself. I often sat alone and dreamed. I would have dreams of graduating from college, landing a career, and marrying the man of my dreams. I wanted four children and a house with a white picket fence. My mother taught me the Word of God. I would always hear her praying for me.

My Conversion

Question: What motivated you to receive Christ as your Savior?

Answer: From age 11 through 13, I would have dreams of chains being around my wrists, but there would always be someone there who would rescue me. I wanted to know more about man, His existence, and how everything around me came into being. All of my life I was in the church, but the church was not in me. I had heard about Jesus but did not know Him personally. I believed that God could save me if I just let Him. So, I confessed Jesus as my Lord and Savior and acknowledged that I was a sinner and needed a Savior. During my darkest hour when I felt all alone and afraid, God drew me to Himself.

My Life after Christ

Question: How did your life change after your conversion?

Answer: I began to experience the presence of God. I finished high school, landed my first job, purchased my first car (paid cash for it), graduated from college, and four years later, I got married. After I got married, my husband became very jealous, abusive, and controlling. I thought that since I met him at church, he would be alright, but it only got worse. It took me a while because I thought maybe he would change or that I could change him. In my dreams, I had created this good life. Even though I had a relationship with Christ, I lived as if the good life depended on me and my good works. Sometimes I would ask myself, why me? What have I done to deserve this misery? Finally, I cried out to God. He heard me and delivered me of all of my fears. I never thought that my marriage would end in a divorce, but God was with me, and He has given me more than I had before.

Conclusion

As I look back over my life, I thank God for my trials. They made me strong and taught me how to depend on Jesus. I learned from this experience to never give up and have faith in the Lord Jesus Christ. He will never leave or forsake you. No matter how strong the chains may be that bind you, Jesus is able to deliver you and set you free. And He who the Son sets free is free indeed!

Question: What scriptures helped you through this situation?

Answer: Isaiah 54:17; John 8:31-36; Philippians 4; Proverbs 3:5-6; Psalm 30:5, 34:19, 46:10, 91; Romans 12:1-2.

FLORENE'S TESTIMONY

I was born in Myles, Mississippi. I had a good childhood and a good relationship with my parents.

My Life Before Christ

Question: How did your non-spiritual state affect your feelings, thoughts, attitudes, or relationships?

Answer: Before my life with Christ, I had no purpose. I would ask myself, why am I here? What does the future hold? I was brought up in the church. My parents taught me the Word of God. During that time, church was not an option; it was a requirement. It was the way of life.

My Conversion

Question: What motivated you to receive Christ as your Savior?

Answer: At age seven, I received Christ as my Lord and Savior. My parents put the fear of God in me at an early age, and I did not want to go to hell.

My Life After Christ

Question: How did your life change after your conversion?

Answer: During that time, I was going to church but for all the wrong reasons. After I became an adult, I grew in my relationship with Christ through prayer and studying the Word of God. I enjoyed it so much that I wanted to spend the rest of my life helping others to be established and to grow in their Christian lives.

Conclusion

I would encourage others to pray that God would lead them to a church family where the Word of God is being taught and to be obedient to Him. Believe that God will do what He said He would do. Trust Him and He will give you peace beyond your own understanding.

Question: What scriptures helped sustain you in this situation?

Answer: John 3:16-18; Philippians 4:6; Proverbs 3:5-6

BEVERLY'S TESTIMONY

I had a happy childhood. I was born in Fairfax, Alabama. Being the middle child, I did not get the glamour that the oldest siblings got.

My Life Before Christ

Question: How did your non-spiritual state affect your feelings, thoughts, attitudes, or relationships?

Answer: Before my life with Christ, I was very sensitive about what people said and did to hurt other people. Sometimes I even became depressed. I would always go to my closet and write poetry. God showed me that my purpose here was not to worry about other people but to serve Him.

My Conversion

Question: What motivated you to receive Christ as your Savior?

Answer: I was always in the church, but my awakening came while sitting in my closet. It was there where I had my first encounter with God. He let me know He would never leave or forsake me. I realized He is omnipresent (everywhere at the same time).

My Life After Christ

Question: How did your life change after your conversion?

Answer: At age 17, I got married and we later relocated to Chicago. I got a job with the Board of Education and worked there for 19 years. For the last ten years, I have traveled to various places doing local, national, and international missions. I have met many people while traveling throughout the various airports. Last year, I went to Jamaica, Mexico, East Africa and made other trips on a national level. Every time I returned home from the mission field, I would get ill and find myself going to the hospital for treatment. Sometimes I was admitted for more than 3 days at a time. One day, when they brought me to my room, I awakened to find I had a roommate. I had all kinds of tubes running through my veins. They kept coming in and out giving me medication, shots, and checking my blood pressure. However, I noticed that the young lady who was sharing my room was always knocked out. They would continuously give her medications that kept her drowsy. I began to focus on her and what she was going through. Though I was sick also, I became more concerned about her. So, one morning during the time she was awake, I introduced myself to her. I began to have a gospel conversation with her. I noticed that after her doctor visited her, she seemed to be distraught. She told me about her illness and that the doctor seemed not to be concerned because she had suffered an aneurysm the previous year. So, she began to cry. My focus was so much on her I forgot my problems. I could not get out of my bed, but I started to sing the song "My Worship Is for Real." Then, I asked her if I could pray with her and she said yes, so I did. On the next day, her son came to visit her. She appeared to feel better and thanked me for praying with her and singing that spiritual song for her. Every time I had a visit from one of my health care professionals, I would sing that song. Later that evening, my doctor visited. She was a young, Black, female doctor from Africa. She told me that my numbers were looking good and I may be able to go home on the next day. I called my husband before he left church to let him know I was being released that Sunday. I also told him about the song I sang. As he was on his way to pick me up, He told me at church, the choir was singing my song: "My Worship Is for Real." That's when I realized that all sickness is not unto death, but sometimes God is setting you up to give Him the glory by going into all the earth preaching, teaching, sharing the good news and praying for people who are in need because it is *all about Him*!

Conclusion

God is a miracle working God. He let me know that this sickness will not end in death. No, it is for God's glory so that He and His Son may be glorified through it (John 11:4). I give God praise, for He is Jehovah Rapha, the God who heals. He deserves the praise. I know without a doubt that God has the power to heal all sicknesses and diseases. There will come a time in your life when you must know Jesus for yourself. He is the great I AM!

Question: What scriptures helped sustain you in this situation?

Answer: Exodus 3:14; Hebrews 13:5; John 11:4

CHRISTOPHER'S TESTIMONY

I was born and raised in New York City, New York.

My Life Before Christ

Question: How did your non-spiritual state affect your feelings, thoughts, attitudes, and relationships?

Answer: I can remember in the 9th grade meeting a friend named Mark at the New York School of printing. We would hang out together and smoke marijuana.

My Conversion

Question: What motivated you to receive Christ as your Savior?

Answer: In my 10th grade year, I noticed a big change in my friend Mark. He was totally changed. He did not have the desire to do the things we used to do. Then he started to have a gospel conversation with me about Jesus. Later, I moved to a different neighborhood. There, I met a family member who led me to the Lord Jesus Christ.

My Life After Christ

Question: How did your life change after your conversion?

Answer: After I received Christ, something happened in my life. Now, I could see what Mark was talking about. Now, my life has purpose. Years later, I moved to Chicago, IL where I continued my journey in the Lord. All my life, I have had a passion for music. As a matter of fact, it runs in my family. The Lord led me to Broadview Missionary Baptist Church where I became the drummer and percussionist. I have served in the music ministry for almost 20 years. On Sunday, February 24, 2019, I went to church (not feeling well) and found myself leaning over the banister. At that time, my chest felt tight, but I was not in pain. After the service began, and I finished jamming for Jesus, I sat down. All of a sudden, I started to sweat as if I was working out in the gym. Blake, the drummer, asked me if I was feeling okay because I looked flush. He told me to go to the back of the church building and get some air. By then, Ernest, the minister of music came out and asked me if I was okay. I said yes, but he knew something was wrong. So, he and Beverly took me to the nurse's station to get my vitals checked. My blood pressure was almost 200. After service was over, they told my wife to take me to the emergency room. I ended up in E.R. at Loyola Medical Center. My blood pressure had risen to 247. The doctors took 3 electrocardiograms (EKG's). The doctors explained to me that I had a heart attack. At that time, I was taken up for more testing. Three veins in my heart were clogged. They took me up for surgery that same night and put in stents where the vein was 95 percent clogged.

Conclusion

God is Jehovah Rapha, (the God who heals). Just like He did it for me, He will do it for you if you trust and obey Him! The next day, the doctors released me. I was able to go to the house of the Lord on Sunday to worship Him. I was back in my position praising Him with the instruments.

Question: What scripture did you stand on during this time of testing?

Answer: Exodus 15:26; Hebrews 13:5; Job 19:25-27; Philippians 4:13

REGINALD'S TESTIMONY

I had a wonderful childhood. I was born in Chicago, Illinois. My relationship with my parents was great. I was an only child.

My Life Before Christ

Question: How did your non-spiritual state affect your feelings, thoughts, attitudes, and relationships?

Answer: Being an only child, I lived a good life. My parents took care of all of my physical needs.

My Conversion

Question: What motivated you to receive Christ as your Savior?

Answer: At age 11, I felt a strong desire to serve Christ. So, I joined the junior choir.

My Life After Christ

Question: How did your life change after your conversion?

Answer: My life had purpose. I wanted to do everything I could please my parents. I served faithfully until age 18. At age 18, I began to backslide. During that time, my life was influenced by peer pressure, which led to more peer pressure. Then, I was intimidated by gangs. This went on for almost 2 years. At age 19, I began to experiment with marijuana, which lasted for 15 years. Then, I began to hang out and do things that were contrary to the Word of God, which resulted in my incarceration.

Question: When did you decide that enough was enough?

Answer: While I was incarcerated, I was convicted because I knew in my heart that what I was doing was not right. My parents had taught me better. Even during my incarceration, God had mercy on me. I began my ministry in Cook County Jail, teaching Bible study.

Conclusion

Question: What advice would you give to others who are struggling in the same area?

Answer: I would tell them to be transparent and trust God by faith. You may not always see it or feel it because this is a faith walk. God knows about your struggles and pain. There is no problem so big or hurt so bad that God cannot deliver. However, you must make up your mind to follow Jesus.

Question: What scriptures helped sustain you in this situation?

Answer: 2 Corinthians 5:7; Jeremiah 29:11

ACKNOWLEDGMENTS

I AM ETERNALLY GRATEFUL TO my Heavenly Father for birthing intercession in me. I am grateful to my Lord and Savior Jesus Christ for giving me the wisdom, knowledge, and understanding to compile this information on prayer. I am also grateful to the Holy Spirit for guiding my mind in such a creative way.

I thank God for my godly parents, Deacon Theodore R. and Callie Elmore. I thank God for the great wisdom of Pastor Emeritus Clarence W. Hopson for laying a solid biblical foundation, and for his wife Lennis. I praise and thank God for Pastor Marvin G. Parker and former Lady Inez who prepared the way for the men of God to walk beside me on the journey. Thanks to Pastor Adron Robinson, Country Club Hills, Illinois, Pastor Bobby L. Palmore, Sr. and Emmanuel Intercessory Prayer Group of Birmingham, Alabama, Rev. Marion Anderson, Bellwood, Illinois, Minister Helen Means, Chicago, Illinois, Apostle Shirley Battles, Minister Tabari, and Chrystal Young of Victoria Texas for seeing something in me, encouraging and praying for me.

Thanks to my professors at Moody Bible Institute: Dr. Cassandra April, Dr. Green, Dr. Sajan Mathews, and Dr. Bill Thrasher for being such strong men and woman of prayer.

Thanks to you, Deacon Harvey Bond, for creating the power points, and to Deacon Larry Tolbert and the administrative staff for all of your support. I thank the educators, writers, and proofreaders: Vanessa Elmore, Debra Harvey, Marcia Hourston, Jacqueline Karriem, Delores Matt, Joyce McClain, Catherine Scott, Linda Woods-Smith, Ada Thompson, and Mary Ann Watts who provided invaluable feedback, insight, and expertise.

Many thanks to Beverly, Christopher, Florene, Reginald, and Yolanda for sharing their testimonies. To the prayer warriors: John Billingsley, Rev. and Sis. Arthur and Eliza Edwards, Cynthia Brown, Diane Cooper, Lenetta Covington, Clem Delane, Jerrell and Latoya Elmore, Minnie Gay, Frankie Howard, Valerie and Rhema King, Jimmie Miller, Ruby and Elicia Nelson, Gloria Pruitt, Tanyka Robinson, Patricia Young, Rev. Vernon and Dorothy Terry, Rev. Lee J. Scott, Rev. Stephen Godfrey, Paula Ward, Chauncey and Joyce Woodson, Lonnie Thomas, Bill Ward, Jason Mathews, Dildra McCarroll, Paulette Cook, Carolyn Johnson, and the Tuesday Bible School, thanks for your love, encouragement, and most importantly, your prayers.

Thanks to the Christian Education Department, Superintendents, Trustees Edward Smith, Jeria Backstrom, Wanda Hicks, Prison/Jail Ministry Rev. Charles and Shelma Pearson, Rev. Darryl Backstrom, Rev. Preston Jordan, Rev. Gerald Coble, Murtle English, Claudette Hendricks, Johnny Hutson, Carlean Nicholson, Deacon Larry Lee and the Pulpit Search Committee, Danielle Bush, Justin Funchess, Dr. Shante Holley, Chris and Kathy Owens, Sonja Williams, Marvin Edwards.

Thanks to Rev. David Swope and the Young Adults, Youths, and Children of BMBC, Missionaries: Eugenia Curry, E. Lynne Johnson, Willie C. and Beverly McLaughlin, Robert and Linda Taylor, and Maxine Smith. Thanks to Lorrie, Larry, and Jeanell Harmon, Deleslie Hunt, Lou Hatton, Bernice Malden, Lee and Patricia Mallett, Kathy Rates, Mission Pastor Robert C. Walker, Matilda Ann Walker and the Missions Prayer Team. Thanks to Deacon Leon and Brunetta Smith, Trustees Anthony Green, Terrence Hunter, and Almeadie Kirkland. Thank you for being a blessing to me through your songs and prayers. I also show much gratitude to Deacon Anthony and Sandra Lumpkin for your professionalism and insight into the original layout, artwork, design, and typesetting.

Special thanks to my wonderful family, my husband, Douglas M. Woods, Sr., my children, Douglas Woods II, Kelvin Donald, Deacon Cledis and my beautiful daughter-in-law Rita Ward, and my loving sister, Vanessa Elmore who supported me from the very beginning. I am most grateful to Interim Pastor Christopher C. Robinson, Sr. and Reverend Dr. Eric A. King for believing in me, walking with me every step of the way, and sharing their wisdom with me during the process. I thank God for their wives, Interim Lady Annette Robinson, and Sister Linda King, who allowed their spouses to meet with me continually for the past two years.

I could not have done it without you. May the Lord bless you all!

BIBLIOGRAPHY

Concordia Publishing House, *My Prayer Book*, 1983.

Cook, Arnold, *Historical Drift, Must My Church Die?* Christian Publication, Inc., 2000, Republished in 2008.

Division of Christian Education of the National Council, *My Prayer Book*, Concordia Publishing House, 1980.

Dunn, Ronald, *Don't Just Stand There, Pray Something, Intercessory Prayer*, Thomas Nelson Publishers, 1992.

Enns, Paul, *The Moody Handbook of Theology*, Moody Press, 1989, Republished 2014 Articles.

Hale, Thomas, Thorson, Steven, *The Applied Old Testament Commentary*, David C. Cook Distribution, 1984.

Hale, Thomas, Thorson, Steven, *The Applied New Testament Commentary*, David C. Cook Distribution, 2012.

Lunsford, Stacey, *Hope is on the Horizon*, Arise, and Shine Production, 2009-10.

McLaughlin, Beverly, *Inside My Sunshine Closet*, Author House Publishers, 2006.

Moody, DL, and Sankey "The Gospel Awakenings, Revival Meetings Prayer Meeting Talks, Conducted by Moody and Sankey," pp.721-733. Published in 1888.

Omartian, Stormie, *The Power of a Praying Nation*, Harvest House Publishers, 2002.

Rydelnik, Michael, Vanlaningham, Michael, *The Moody Bible Commentary*, Moody Publishers, 2014.

Thrasher, Bill, *Victorious Praying*, Moody Publishers, Lockman Foundation Moody Bible Institute Classroom Notes, 1995.

Weymann Dorothy Mason, *Thus Saith God's Word, Scripture Aids for Counseling*, M.D. Production Publishers, 1988.

Websites

https://www.hillcrestweb.org › sermon-speaker › rev-dr-adron-robinson

https://www.cph.org › p-112-My-Prayer-Book

https://www.emmanuel7.org

https://www.gotquestions.org/steps-to-salvation.html

https://www.prayingscriptures.com/nations.shtml

Made in the USA
Middletown, DE
28 July 2022